Anonymous

Sherman's Bar Harbor Guide

Business Directory And Reference Book

Anonymous

Sherman's Bar Harbor Guide
Business Directory And Reference Book

ISBN/EAN: 9783744733748

Printed in Europe, USA, Canada, Australia, Japan

Cover: Foto ©Andreas Hilbeck / pixelio.de

More available books at **www.hansebooks.com**

BAR HARBOR AND BOSTON.

Steamship communication between landings in Penobscot Bay and Boston was first established in 1824, the steamers now plying between Rockland and Boston are,

PENOBSCOT,
CAPT. OTIS INGRAHAM, Master.

KATAHDIN,
CAPT. MARCUS PIERCE, : : Master.

LEWISTON,
CAPT. MARK L. INGRAHAM, : : Master.

These connect at Rockland with the side-wheel, capacious, saloon

STEAMER MT. DESERT,
CAPT. WILLIAM C. SAWTELLE, : : Master.

To and from Bar Harbor, and other landings on the Island of Mount Desert.

The steamers are fast, large and commodious, the saloons and staterooms finely fitted and furnished, and are fitted with every appliance for the comfort, convenience and safety of passengers.

During the season of summer travel steamers leave Bar Harbor at one o'clock, P. M., and Boston at 5 P. M., daily except Sunday.

Officers and employees are courteous and polite, and the cuisine is of acknowledged excellence.

BOSTON & BANGOR STEAMSHIP CO.

E. S. J. MORSE, Agent, Bar Harbor.
WILLIAM H. HILL, President and Gen. Manager, Boston.

SHERMAN'S

Bar Harbor Guide,

Business Directory and

Reference Book.

PUBLISHED BY

W. H. SHERMAN.

Copyright, 1890.
[All Rights Reserved.]

There is only one Bar Harbor.—[James G. Blaine.

BAR HARBOR, ME.
BAR HARBOR PRESS CO. PRINT.
1890

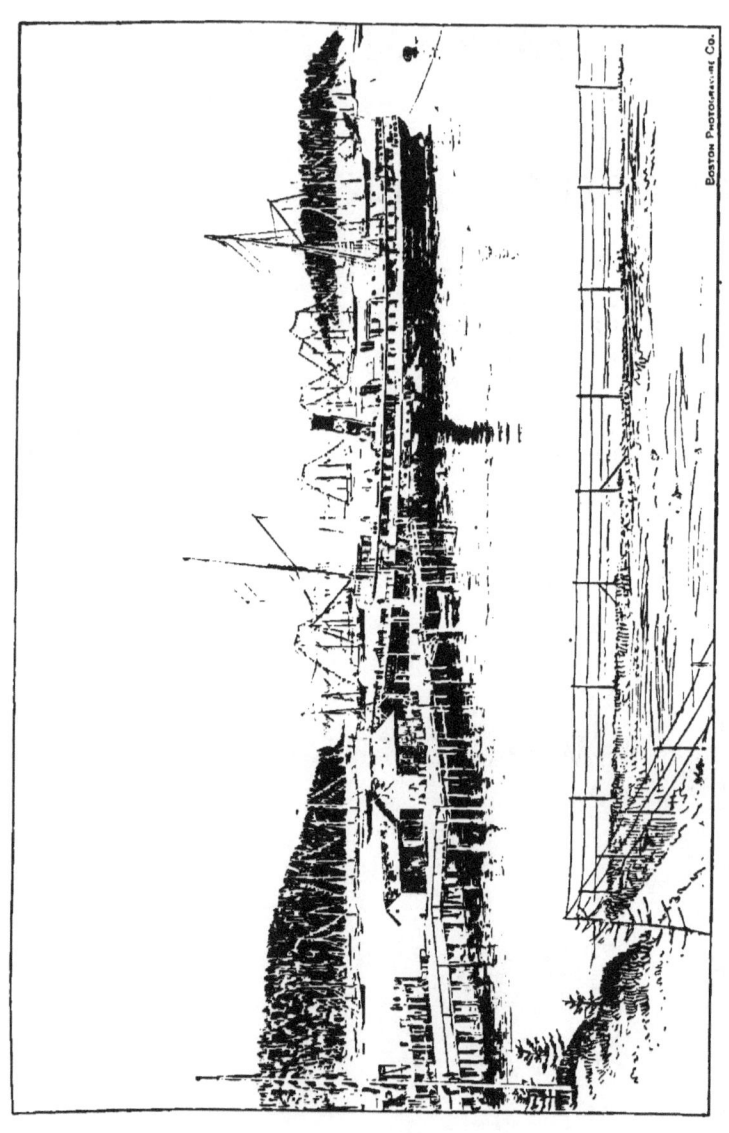

VIEW FROM THE NEWPORT HOUSE VERANDAH, SHOWING THE YACHT FLEET AND THE STEAMSHIP OLIVETTE.

✻ INTRODUCTION. ✻

In past years Bar Harbor has left to the enterprise and the pen of strangers the grateful task of bringing her accommodations and attractions before the public. The result of this "foreign" advertising has been that nearly all the so-called guide-books of Mount Desert have been devoted principally to the interests of the concerns which published them, while Bar Harbor and its interests have occupied only a secondary place therein.

The aim of this little book, published solely by subscription of the citizens of Bar Harbor, is to give the traveling public a concise and, if possible, an impartial account of the attractions of this village as a summer resort, free from any advertising intent save that which has the interest of the entire community in view. It is proposed also to make this a book of reference to which the tourist may apply for information on any point connected with the summer life of the village; and where the would-be visitor may find or estimate the cost of living, either in hotel or cottage.

Somehow the impression has been conveyed to the public that Bar Harbor is totally destitute of any conveniences in the shape of first class stores; and it has been no uncommon thing in past years for cottagers, visiting the village for the first time, to send ahead of them a vessel-load of groceries and furniture. It will be a part of the purpose of this pamphlet to disabuse the public mind in this respect, and to show that all the luxuries as well as the necessaries of life can be procured as readily and cheaply in Bar Harbor as in the city.

Many people are deterred from visiting Bar Harbor by the idea that there is a tedious, uncomfortable and expensive trip, by land or water, between them and this paradise of summer resorts: this work will strive to show them that they can travel cheaply, rapidly and luxuriously in the most modern of steamboats or palace cars. In fine, it will be the endeavor of the editor to correct all those erroneous notions about Bar Harbor life which have sprung rather from a lack of information than from misstatement; and to illumine the path thither in a manner that, it is hoped, will lead many to tread it to their lasting benefit, during the coming summer.

It is with a deep sense of his inability to depict attractions to which the talent of even the greatest of modern artists has failed to do full justice, that the writer begins his task. But he is comforted in the reflection that those of his readers to whom the scenery is familiar can fully appreciate the difficulties of the work, while those for whom the future still holds the pleasure, will forget the feeble copy in the contemplation of the sublime reality.

ALICK J. GRANT.

A Bird's-eye View of Bar Harbor and Frenchman's Bay.

* * *

A beautiful, landlocked bay stretching away into the distance and losing itself in numerous coves and inlets, amid purple hills and green, wooded shores, its waters now washing the feet of weather-worn precipices and anon breaking softly on glistening sand and pebbles. Studded over the surface of this bay are bright emerald islands, rich in foliage, stately landmarks of the ages. As the summer sun shines brightly on this panorama of sea and mountain, one can imagine himself in the home of the lotus eaters, so enticingly does it seem to invite to repose.

On one side of this beautiful bay is an island, an island rich in all the wonders and beauties of nature. Majestic mountains rear their bold summits toward the sky, and sheltered valleys lie nestling at their base. Lovely lakes abound, reflecting in their pellucid depths an endless vista of mountain and forest. Brooks, with shady pools where the trout love to hide, flow gently through its vales, or leap, foaming, from rock to rock in their headlong course to the sea. Mountain, forest and lake scenery meet the eye in every direction, while the rock-bound shores and lofty cliffs form a picturesque frontier to this island paradise.

Once the red man roved these forests and chased the deer on these mountain sides. Once the stem of his bark canoe breasted the waters of these lakes, and the smoke of his wigwam ascended from the leafy vales. Now, the scene is changed. The march of progress and civilization has driven these denizens of the forest further and further from their former haunts, till but a few scattered remnants are left of this once powerful people.

The natural beauties of this wonderful island have been recognized and taken advantage of by civilized man. Look at that landlocked bay now! A cooling breeze ripples the surface of the water, bearing health and comfort to the weary toiler from the crowded city and bringing the bloom to the cheek of the devotee of fashion, surfeited with the gaiety of the past winter. Magnificent steamers ply on its waters and stately yachts ride at anchor in its harbors. White-winged boats skim across its surface, laden with pleasure parties whose only object seems to be to drown dull care and live in the glories of the present.

At the base of the highest mountain on the island, on a plateau environed by wooded heights, with the blue waters washing its shores, stands a city of palaces. Magnificent hotels rear their lofty turrets in the air; and palatial residences are embowered amid the woods by the shore, or are perched like eyries upon the cliffs and hillsides. A fine steamboat wharf projects into the waters of the bay. The streets of this summer city are wide, and in good order. Commodious, well-equipped stores offer their wares to the passers-by. Stately edifices, beautiful as wealth and art can render them, afford an opportunity to people of all denominations to worship God after the manner of their fathers. Club-houses, rich in architectural beauties and redolent of fashion and the beau-monde, cater to the tastes of the wealthy and fastidious. The sanitary arrangements are the finest that skill and money can provide; and no expense has been spared in conducing to the comfort of the many thousands who annually visit this island.

A network of fine roads covers the island, opening up to the tourist its beautiful woodland and lake scenery. Small bridle-paths penetrate its innermost recesses, leading the artist to his favorite haunts and the angler to the scenes of his sport. On other parts of the island the same progress and development may be noticed. Many fine building sites have been opened up by the numerous roads, and lovely villas are springing up on hillside and in valley. Smaller summer resorts are growing into notoriety at other points on the island; and the day is not far distant when Mount Desert island will be one vast summer resort.

This, gentle reader, is but a distant view: details are yet to try your patience and impart information. But first let us withdraw the curtain which shrouds the past, and endeavor to trace the rise and progress of civilization on this beautiful island. Who were the first Mount Desert "rusticators"?

From "Bar Harbor Days." Copyright, 1887, by Harper & Brothers

THUNDER CAVE, ON THE CELEBRATED OCEAN DRIVE.

Discovery ✺ of ✺ Mount ✺ Desert.

* * *

Nearly two hundred and fifty years ago, the French navigator, Champlain, struck by the barren grandeur of Mount Desert's mountain peaks, entered in his log-book the words "L'isle des Monts Deserts." How little did the wearied mariner dream of the future greatness of this island, as he battled with the elements off its surf-beaten shores. To him it was a coast to be avoided— fraught with unknown perils, perhaps peopled by barbarous enemies. Nevertheless Champlain gave to the world the first authentic account of America's famous watering place, and paved the way for its first civilized visitors.

Henry IV of France, in 1603, had granted to his "Well beloved Sieur De Monts, in ordinary of his best chamber, the territory known as Acadia, described as extending from the 40th to the 46th degree of north latitude;" and this nobleman, for the purpose of taking possession of his newly acquired property, had fitted out two vessels, and, with Champlain as pilot, had sailed for the unknown West. Having established a settlement and erected a fort on St. Croix island, Champlain, in a *pattache* of seventeen tons, with twelve sailors and two savages as guides, started on a voyage of exploration along the coast. It was during this voyage that he made the following entries in his log-book.

He says: "September 5th, we passed also near to an island about four or five leagues long, in the neighborhood of which we just escaped being lost on a little rock on a level with the water, which made an opening in our bark near the keel. From this island to the main land on the north, the distance is less than a hundred paces. It is very high, and notched in places so that there is an appearance to one at sea as of seven or eight mountains extending along near each other. The summit of the most of them is destitute of trees as there are only rocks on them. The woods consist of pines, firs and birches only. I named it Isle des Monts Deserts. The latitude is 44:30."

Champlain and De Monts returned to France in 1607, having claimed the whole of the explored region for that country; and De Monts transferred the grant of land to Madame de Guerchville. This grant was confirmed by the king.

Madame de Guerchville, a religious enthusiast whose confessors were Jesuits, conceived the idea of converting the heathen who undoubtedly inhabited this her Western territory; and with this end in view, on the 12th of March, 1613, a vessel of one hundred tons, with forty-eight colonists and sailors and two Jesuit priests, Fathers Quentin and Du Thet, set sail from Honfleur for the coast of Maine. She was commanded by a French courtier named Saussaye. On the 16th of May they touched at La Heve, and then passing on to Port Royal they took on board Fathers Biard and Masse and sailed for the mouth of the Penobscot river.

Off the southeastern coast of the Island of Menan they were overtaken by a thick fog, so that for forty-eight hours they were entirely at fault as to the ship's position. On the evening of the second day it cleared away so that they could see the stars, and when morning dawned they found themselves near the cliffs of Mount Desert, an island which the natives called Pemetic. With a fair wind the ship entered Frenchman's Bay and anchored in a harbor on the east side of the island. From this place they travelled three leagues westward to the place which they made the site of their colony. The ship was brought round to this spot and the colonists disembarked.

In his journal Father Biard describes the site as follows: "This place is a beautiful hill, sloping gently from the sea shore and supplied with water by a spring on either side. It fronts the south and east towards Pentagoet bay. The port and harbor are the finest possible, in a position commanding the entire coast: the harbor especially is as smooth as a pond, being shut in by the large island of Mount Desert, besides being surrounded by certain small islands which break the force of the winds and waves and fortify the entrance. It is large enough to hold any fleet, and is navigable for the largest ship up to within a cable's length from the shore."

No one acquainted with the topography of Mount Desert can fail to recognize, in this description, the spot now known as Fernald's Point, at Southwest Harbor. There the French springs are still to be seen, and some ancient cellars, presumably of French origin. In the valley connected at the north are ranges of cellars still pointed out, and the oldest inhabitants claim to have seen pieces of crockery lying about them in the days of their childhood.

Here they were visited by Indians who had an encampment near the spot, and Father Biard did good missionary work among them, baptizing their chief Asticou. But all was not harmony in this little settlement. A mutiny broke out among the sailors. The agreement on their joining the expedition was that they should stay three months after their arrival in any port in Acadia, and they claimed that the three months dated from their touching at La Heve; the pilot, Flory, took their part. La Saussaye maintained the contrary and said that their engagement should be dated from their landing on Mount Desert. Besides, La Saussaye was desirous of attending to agriculture, while the others wished to build dwellings and fortifications.

In the meanwhile an enemy was approaching who would settle their disputes in a very peremptory manner. Samuel Argall, the English governor of South Virginia, fitted out an armed vessel and sailed, in May, for the coast of Maine to fish for cod. Encountering heavy fogs, he at last found himself near Penobscot Bay. Here he was boarded by Indians who by signs gave him to understand that there was a French colony somewhere in the neighborhood.

To a man of Argall's stamp, nothing in the way of booty came amiss: and he would just as soon catch Frenchmen as cod. He learned the numbers, and strength of the colony from the Indians, and keeping one of them as a pilot, steered for Mount Desert. Biard's narrative excuses the perfidy of the Indians by saying that they mistook the English for friends of the Frenchmen, who were in search of them. Be this as it may, the French garrison were greatly surprised one morning, in the midst of their disputes, to see a strange vessel heading in towards the shore under a cloud of canvas, with a blood-red flag at her mast-head and a row of frowning cannon on each side.

Du Thet, with a few of the bravest of the band, hastened aboard their vessel, but had no time to get their anchor up. Argall bore down on them, firing a broadside as he came along. The Jesuit Du Thet himself applied the match to a cannon, but, as he was no artillerist, his shot flew wide of the mark. A volley of musketry from the English, and Du Thet was shot down. Argall fired into the French vessel again and again, and then lowering a boat, boarded her, to find the crew dead or severely wounded. The English landed and pillaged the settlement. La Saussaye had fled to the woods. Argall broke open his chest, took thence his commissions and royal letters and closed it again. The next day La Saussaye presented himself in camp. The English captain demanded his commission. Saussaye could not find it and was immediately branded as an imposter and robber, and the surviving French were all made prisoners. Such was the end of Jesuit rule on Mount Desert.

Of the aborigines but few descendants are left in this state. The Penobscot Indians live at Oldtown, and the Passamaquoddy at Eastport. In summer a few members of these tribes form a small colony at Bar Harbor, and make a living by the sale of such novelties as grass baskets, slippers and bead-work to the summer visitors. Traces of these former settlers are still to be found in great abundance on the island of Mount Desert and along the shores of Frenchman's Bay. At East Lamoine, where the action of the waves has gradually washed away the banks, heaps of clam shells have been found containing arrow heads, stone hatchets and the bones of birds and animals which have been used for food. Among these remains are bones of the moose, bear and deer. On Bar Island, at Fernald's Point and

Hull's Cove are to be seen more traces of such gigantic clambakes; and where the plough has broken the soil for the first time, the ground has been found literally whitened with the remains of these Indian dinners.

The visitor, if of an archæological turn of mind, will derive much pleasure from a visit to those ancient shell heaps. Prof. Henry W. Haynes of Boston, who has been a guest at the Newport Hotel, Bar Harbor, for many years, is an enthusiastic searcher among these musty relics, and never leaves Mount Desert without a rare collection of Indian remains gathered from the scene of his summer sojourn. For those who prefer the Red Man, living, to his shades, the Indian summer encampment at Bar Harbor will have its charms; and really the fancy work of these dusky sons and daughters of the forest is well worth the price paid for it.

Rev. O. H. Fernald of Bucksport, a native of Mount Desert, in an interesting article on the island, suggests that it may have been first discovered by the Norsemen. There is no doubt that these old sea-kings visited the New England coast in the eleventh century, as traces of their occupation are still to be found at Newport and Fall River. Mr. Fernald, in the article above mentioned, writes as follows:

"At Southwest Harbor, one-half mile inland on high ground, there has been a clearing from time immemorial. If we are correct in our position it was there ere the French settled at Fernald's Point in A. D. 1613; and about it seems to be marks as if fortified by a stockade; but in those early time a stockade must have meant European occupancy.

"On Fernald's Point, and near the shore, is a well which has been of long standing. It differs from our habit since it seems to be stoned up in a triangular section, though now caving in. Query: Is it of Norse origin?

"About A. D. 1830 there was dug up on the east bank of Somes Sound opposite Fernald's Point, the jaw bone of a man which the writer of this article claims must have belonged to a person eight feet high. And some twenty years since while taking a geological survey of the island, a gentleman informed me that in deepening his cellar a few years previous he dug into the graves of the dead, and took out several skulls of giants. Query: Were they not Norsemen?

"I had hoped that ruins and inscriptions in the Runic language might be found on our rocks; but afterwards learned that the disintegration of Mount Desert granite was such as to obliterate all inscriptions in less than fifty years. What then could I hope for after the erosion of rainfall and frost for nine centuries?"

From "Bar Harbor Days." Copyright, 1887, by Harper & Brothers.

A GALA-DAY AT BAR HARBOR.

The ✻ Second ✻ French ✻ Grant.

※ ※ ※

From the destruction of the little colony of Jesuits at Fernald's Point, nothing of interest in connection with Mount Desert appears in history until A. D. 1688, when we learn that the French King, in recognition of important military services rendered in America, granted to Antonie de la Motte Cadillac the whole of Mount Desert and some of the adjacent islands. Cadillac died about the year 1719 without having taken possession of his estate; but in 1786 his granddaughter, Madame Marie Therese de Gregoire, and her husband Bartholomy de Gregoire came over from France and laid claim to the property. Lafayette and Thomas Jefferson interested themselves in their favor, and, as the Government were favorably disposed to France and her people, the General Court of Massachusetts, in June, 1787, granted to them "all such parts and parcels of the Island of Mount Desert and the other islands and tracts of land particularly described in the grant or patent of his late most Christian Majesty Louis XIV, to said Monsieur de la Motte Cadillac which now remain the property of this Commonwealth whether by original right, cession, confiscation or forfeiture, to hold all the aforesaid parts and parcels of the said lands and islands to them the said Monsieur and Madame de Gregoire, their heirs and assigns forever." This grant was subject to certain reservations and to the rights of actual settlers. On this nearly all the titles to real estate on the island are based. The family were naturalized by special act of the Legislature.

The whole eastern part of the island, with the exception of

those lots already occupied by squatters thus became the property of the De Gregoires; and they took up their abode at Hulls Cove, a little settlement a couple of miles to the northward of Bar Harbor. Here they lived, loved and respected by the rude fishermen who surrounded them, until their death about 1810. A small wooden cross in the little graveyard at Hull's Cove marks the last resting place of this old French couple; and the remains of the cellar of their house are still pointed out to visitors. Their children returned to their native land. The vast property (about 60,000 acres) had to be sold for the de Gregoires' support, and at their death every acre of their great heritage had departed from them. A subscription has been set on foot lately by the Bar Harbor RECORD to place a monument over their grave; and it is probable that a granite shaft will soon indicate to the tourist the spot where the original grantors of Bar Harbor real estate titles lived and died.

A Tow Path Scene.

Birth of a Summer Resort.

* * *

What a contrast between the Mount Desert of to-day and the *terra incognita* of the Jesuit missionaries! Where Fathers Biard and Masse preached the "glad tidings" to the aborigines of the island, is now a populous village thronged during summer with merry crowds of fashionable pilgrims on a pleasure crusade.

Perhaps the ashes of the martyr Du Thet are mingled with the remains of last season's festive clam bake. On the waters of the harbor once ploughed by the keel of the pirate Argal's frigate, now ride stately yachts and palatial steamers. Probably the very stones of which the French cellars were built, now form the underpinning of some of the summer hotels.

The hills which once echoed the hymns of praise from the pious throats of the brethren of Jesus, now resound with the joyous mirth of the picnic. But the same grim old mountains—hoary-headed sentinels—still look down upon the scene; and the everlasting ocean hurls its thunderous surf upon the shore or gently kisses the pebbly beach as it did two hundred and fifty years ago.

But if the changes wrought since the beginning of the seventeenth century are wonderful, how much more so are those comprised within the comparatively short period since the year 1825. Bar Harbor was then but a little fishing and ship-building community, and the plateau from Duck Brook to Cromwell's Harbor was sparsely dotted with small farms. Its inhabitants were few in number and simple in manner of living. How little they recked of what the future might have in store for this island home of theirs! No visions of lordly mansions disturbed their thoughts as they tilled the little plot which supplied their table. No towering hotel with its long corridors and handsome suites of apartments rose up before their minds' eye. No flash of electric lights lit up for them the gloomy caverns of the future. They ploughed the furrow, mended their nets, felled the timber and built their fishing vessels, for the present: the future, with its telephones and electric lighting, its palatial hotels and handsome residences, disturbed them not for they could not conceive it.

Probably the first settler at Bar Harbor was a man named Nicholas Thomas, who lived on what is now known as Birch Point. In 1825 the only store in town was situated on the shore near where the steamboat wharf now stands, and was kept by a man named "Glasseye Brown." The stock was brought from the westward in vessels, boated ashore and carried up the beach. Prior to 1855 ship building was the chief industry. The large pine trees used in the business were cut in the neighborhood of the present Acadia Club House, and were hauled to where the bowling alley now stands and cut up with a whip saw. The principal families then were the Higgins, Wasgatts, Hamors, Rodicks and Roberts. In the summer of 1850 the artist, Church, visited the island, and boarded with Albert Higgins the proprietor of the Harbor House, which then stood very near its present location. In 1855, part of the Agamont House (burned about two years ago) was built on Main street by Tobias Roberts. A few Bangor people and artists used to board there. Capt. James Hamor's farm included the present site of the Rodick House, and the farm house stood near Cottage street. The old Higgins' homestead was near the corner of Main and Cottage streets, and the barn occupied the site of the present Mount Desert Block. There were only two houses between Eddy's Brook and Duck Brook, and the forests extended to Kebo street.

The steamer Lewiston landed passengers and freight in summer between the months of June and September, Captain Deering himself engineering the first steamboat wharf. A little later the Rodicks built two cottages, and then the Deering House was built in 1858. The late Mr. Alpheus Hardy of Boston was one of the first non-resident property owners. He purchased Birch

Point from "Uncle" Stephen Higgins in 1868 for $300, and built the first cottage on that spot. The Weld and Minot lots were soon after purchased for $2500, and the Ogden property at Cromwell's Harbor, (now Mr. Geo. W. Vanderbilt's estate), was bought about the same time. The old White Church was raised in 1855, but was not finished for some years.

The artists who had made the village their summer home, took away with them sketches of the beautiful scenery of the island; and slowly but surely Mount Desert crept toward notoriety. Where once the proud trees bowed and fell to the woodman's axe, handsome summer residences grew up as if by enchantment; the shores, which once echoed to the strokes of the ship carpenter's mallet, began to be the scene of busy traffic. The bay, once a promising field for porgie fishermen, soon became dotted in summer time with a variety of crafts, from the tiny canoe to the stately yacht. Along its rocky shores where the children of former generations had rambled in their long vacation, and perhaps where smugglers once landed their store of contraband goods, there soon flocked many gay pleasure seekers. Then, as though by the wave of an enchanter's wand, in one glad summer the gay transformation scene was enacted, and Bar Harbor stood revealed to the world in her true character as the Queen of American Summer Resorts.

And yet all these changes, startling as they are in themselves, are but the result of the natural attractions of the island graphically represented by the pencils of world-renowned artists, and carefully fostered by the encouraging hands of industry and perseverance.

VIEW OF BAR HARBOR FROM RODICK'S ISLAND.

General * Description.

* * *

Bar Harbor, in the town of Eden, occupies a narrow irregular plateau in the northeastern section of the island of Mount Desert, Hancock county, Maine. The northern boundary of this plateau is a little stream known as Duck Brook, the southern is Newport Mountain: westward a chain of hills—Strawberry Hill, Mount Kebo and Great Pond Hill—cut it off from the remainder of the island, while the eastern front of the plateau rests on Frenchman's Bay.

The middle third of this plateau contains the village proper. It is laid out quite regularly, the main street running almost due north and south with the others cutting it at right angles. Off the northern front of the village is Bar Island (or Rodick's Island as it is called after the owners) connected with it by a bar which is dry at low water and forms a good carriage drive. Stretching out to the eastward from this point, across the bay, is a chain of small rocky islands known as the PORCUPINES from their fancied resemblance to that animal. The eastern side of the village looks on Frenchman's Bay, and the southern is bounded by a small stream called CROMWELL'S HARBOR brook. Westward Malden Hill, Little Kebo and a low wooded hill comprising the district known as Abby's Retreat, look down on the village. The northern and southern portions of the plateau are the suburbs of Bar Harbor, and contain most of the beautiful summer residences for which the place is deservedly famous. These will be taken up later, after the village has been described.

MAIN STREET, as already stated, runs nearly due north and south on the eastern side of the village, its greatest distance from the sea being not over one-third of a mile, while towards its northern extremity it is much nearer. To the north it terminates in WEST STREET within a few rods of the Maine Central Steamboat wharf. Following it in a southerly direction leads one to the OTTER CREEK and SCHOONER HEAD roads. From Main street, easterly, numerous smaller streets and lanes lead to a walk along the shore of the Bay—the TOW PATH as it is called, of which more hereafter.

Main street is the principal business street of the town, and several large blocks are built on it besides a few hotels. Within a few rods of the wharf, on the eastern side, is the MARLBOROUGH HOTEL: next it is the MOUNT DESERT BLOCK, a large brick building containing doctors' and lawyers' offices, a bank, and the office and press-room of the Bar Harbor Record. Opposite the Marlborough is the office of the Mount Desert Herald. Proceeding south, the next building on the eastern side of the street is the BRADLEY BLOCK, a large building devoted to stores and offices. Opposite this is the RODICK HOUSE, Maine's largest hostelry. Beyond the Bradley block is the BUNKER BLOCK with more stores and offices, and between the blocks is the Bar Harbor Tourist printing office. Still further south, after passing numerous stores, among which is SPROUL's famous restaurant, we come to the HAMOR BLOCK; and opposite to this, on the corner of Main and Mount Desert streets, is the GRAND CENTRAL HOTEL. Beyond the Hamor Block is a row of handsome business blocks, terminating with the PORCUPINE, a commodious apartment house. Next to it is the PORCUPINE RESTAURANT. Here the houses grow scarcer; but after an interval we reach ATLANTIC AVENUE which tends easterly towards the shore and on which is situated the LOUISBURG, one of Bar Harbor's most elegant hotels.

Nearly opposite the Main street end of Atlantic avenue, is the HOTEL DES ISLE, standing back from the street with a large lawn in front of it. South of Atlantic avenue are HANCOCK STREET and then WAYMAN LANE, both of them running easterly towards the Bay shore, but the latter leading to summer residences in the suburbs. On the opposite side of Main street from Wayman Lane, are FIRST and SECOND SOUTH streets and EDGEWOOD street. On the last named is the Electric Light Station. These streets extend to SCHOOL street (a short street running parallel with Main street) and thence connect with some new streets lately built to open up desirable land in the south-western section of the village.

South of this point the village proper ceases, and Main street becomes the SCHOONER HEAD Road. About a mile out the road branches, one part leading down through the Gorge to Otter Creek, the other continuing on to Schooner Head. Within the past two years the Schooner Head Road, which to that date had been a *cul de sac*, has been continued on round the shore, past GREAT HEAD and THUNDER CAVE, to a connection with a branch of the other road at OTTER CLIFFS; and a short cross cut from the latter branch brings the traveler into the main Otter Creek road, near the village of OTTER CREEK. The further course of this road will come, more appropriately, under the head of drives, and will be treated of later.

To return to the streets, after Main street, the first in order, commencing at the steamboat wharf, which is really the gate of Bar Harbor, and working southward, is WEST STREET. This street begins at the Maine Central wharf and runs nearly due west to Eden street, meeting Main street at right angles only a few rods from the wharf. Looking down on it, just above the wharf, is the ROCKAWAY HOUSE, and, almost in the rear of it, the NEWPORT HOTEL. Both of these houses command a fine view of the Bay. Before reaching Main street, on the side of West street facing the harbor, are the boat wharves where every kind of boats, from the tiny birch bark canoe to the handsome steam yacht, can be hired by the hour, day or season. These wharves have floating stages with hinged steps, so that the boats can be reached at any stage of the tide.

On the corner of West and Main streets is the Brewer Hotel, an all-the year-round house, very handy for travelers or transient

guests in summer or winter. From this point to RODERICK
STREET, about two hundred yards west, on the south side of the
street, West street is devoted to stores and restaurants on the
south and wharves on the water side. On the latter side are also
a laundry and a bath house. Roderick street runs south about
two hundred yards and connects with COTTAGE street, a street
parallel to West street.

Following West street a little further we come on the south, to
the WEST END Hotel, surrounded by pretty lawns studded with

MOUNT DESERT READING ROOM.

fountains and rockeries. The next street to the westward, crossing West parallel to Roderick street, is BRIDGE STREET, also
leading to Cottage street on the south. The northern continuation
of this street leads to the BAR, which, as we have already stated,
forms a roadway to Bar Island at low tide. From this point,
westward to HOLLAND AVENUE, West street is bordered on either
side by private grounds and residences.

Formerly this street ended at Holland avenue; but last year the
town laid out and built an extension connecting with Eden street.
This piece of road is wide and level, crossing the creek at the

mouth of Eddy's brook on a wooden bridge with concrete sidewalks; and it opens up some fine sites which will probably be built upon ere long. West street, from the Maine Central wharf to Eden street, is nearly two-thirds of a mile in length; and the portion from the West End Hotel to Eden street commands a fine view of Frenchman's Bay and the northeastern shores of the island.

The next street in order, going south, is COTTAGE STREET, which leaves Main street at the Marlborough Hotel and runs westerly, parallel to West street, to Eden street. On the corner of the two streets next the wharf, is the RODICK BLOCK, a large building occupied by offices with a bank and stores on the first floor. In the opposite corner is the Rodick House lawn. About half way between Main and Roderick streets, on the right hand side of Cottage street, is the cottage of Dr. Morris Longstreth of Philadelphia. Just beyond his house is the POST OFFICE. On the further corner of Roderick street are a couple of stores, nearly the only ones on Cottage street. Most of the street is bordered by private houses, (chiefly of the natives,) with here and there a blacksmith's shop, a carriage shop, or a livery stable. About four hundred yards from Main street, HIGH STREET turns off to the south, connecting with MOUNT DESERT STREET which is parallel to Cottage. On High street is located the HIGH SCHOOL building. Bridge street and Holland avenue cross it in succession, and then Cottage street meets with Eden street at its western end.

Mount Desert street leaves Main street opposite the Porcupine Block, about five hundred yards from the wharf, and runs nearly due West. On the lower corner (towards Cottage street) is the GRAND CENTRAL HOTEL with wide lawns fronting on both streets. A couple hundred yards from the corner is the only store on this street; and just beyond it on the same side (the north) is the beautiful CONGREGATIONAL CHURCH. Opposite the church SCHOOL STREET begins and runs south through the new extension to STRAWBERRY HILL ROAD. On the right hand side of School street, a short distance from Mount Desert, is a handsome brick church built by the METHODIST society. Still further south on School street is the HAMILTON HOTEL, a small, transient house;

and beyond that, the public school building. On the corner of School and Mount Desert streets is the PUBLIC LIBRARY.

A little further along Mount Desert street is the handsome stone church of ST. SAVIOUR, the Episcopal place of worship. Moving westward, we pass High street on the right and come to LEDGE LAWN AVENUE on the left hand. The latter is comparatively a new street, and, running south, opens up a great number of fine building sites in that part of the village. It is wide and well built, and its eastern side is occupied by numerous pretty houses. On that side, about three hundred yards from Mount Desert street, is the BAPTIST CHURCH, a handsome edifice; and a few rods nearer Mount Desert street, on the opposite side, stands the UNITARIAN MEETING-HOUSE, a quaint building. On the western side of the avenue is Miss Mary Shannon's beautiful estate, LEDGE LAWN, which also borders on Mount Desert street, and, further along, on SPRING STREET parallel to Ledge Lawn avenue. The house on this estate is situated on a rocky eminence overlooking Mount Desert street.

A few rods beyond Ledge Lawn avenue is the ST. SAUVEUR HOTEL, on the north side of Mount Desert street; and next to the westward stands the LYNAM HOUSE. From thence to its junction with Eden street, the north side is entirely occupied by cottages.

On the south side of the street, beyond the Lynam House, are two small lanes leading south to a wooded eminence on which are built the summer residences of Dr. Robert Amory, Dr. A. L. Mason and Mrs. James S. Amory, all of Boston. Between the entrance to these lanes and Eden street, are several cottages, the apartment houses known as the PARKER COTTAGES, and the BELMONT HOTEL. It is barely half a mile from Main street along Mount Desert to Eden street; but the fine smooth roadway makes it the popular driving street of the village.

EDEN STREET, beginning at the western end of Mount Desert street and trending north-westerly along the shore of the Bay at an average distance of about a fourth of a mile from it, is the next street of importance, though the greater part of it lies rather in the suburbs than in the village proper. It crosses the western end of both Cottage and West streets also, and just after it passes the latter street dips down into the valley formed by EDDY'S BROOK, so called. Near this point are a few stores; but the houses on it are principally non-resident cottages, and will be taken up later when we come to review the summer residences.

The extension of Eden street, beyond Mount Desert street to the southward, is known as KEBO STREET. On the eastern side of this street, about two hundred yards from the corner of Mount Desert street, stands the Malvern Hotel. Just beyond this is the Roman Catholic chapel, ST. SILVIA'S. Overlooking the street on the west side is a high wooded hill known as Malden Hill, and on this and along the line of the street are many fine cottages which will be mentioned hereafter.

Running west from Mount Desert street, over the high land in that direction, and almost a continuation of that street, is the EAGLE LAKE ROAD, so called. Here also are many handsome cottages to which reference will be made on another page, as also the Casino, the great society resort of Bar Harbor.

In these few pages the writer has endeavored to give the visitor a description of the streets with the location of the principal buildings thereon. A detailed account of the churches, hotels, places of business and cottages will follow; but it is hoped that the above, with the aid of the map, will make the reader familiar with the general outline of the village.

"DEVILSTONE" COTTAGE, SHOWING THE VANDERBILT FAMILY STARTING OUT FOR A BUCKBOARD RIDE.

Amusements.

* * *

THEIR VARIETY.

Everyone has his own idea of pleasure, and it must be a scene of many and varied attractions that will please all. Bar Harbor comes as near affording universal satisfaction to humanity's craving for happiness as any place in this terrestrial sphere possibly can. Nowhere is there a better field for enjoyment than in this little Eden.

Some people there are whose life is a burden to them unless they can pass it in the whirl of society, wearing themselves out with dancing, surfeiting themselves with the good things of the table, turning night into day and using the day for the purposes of the night. There are others again whose tastes are entirely different or whose means will not allow them to keep pace with the fashionable element. For all and each of these Bar Harbor has her peculiar charms.

It has been reported that Bar Harbor has grown into an ultra-fashionable resort; and that instead of being a place of rest for those wearied with the toils or gayeties of winter life in the crowded city, it has become a giddy vortex of society where the day is prolonged into the night of ball and rout, and day itself is but a restless endeavor to get ready for the next night's dissipation. Many whose ideas of pleasure are contrary to this, have been led to suppose that there could be no happiness for them here and have thus been deterred from coming.

But this is a great mistake! Bar Harbor doubtless presents many attractions to the votary of fashion; but they are artificial ones, the product of society itself, such as might be presented anywhere that the gay and fashionable resort. They are apart from and do not interfere with the grand natural attractions of the place and the enjoyment of them. These last are free to all. No fashionable clique can appropriate them to its individual use. Nature, with a lavish hand, has endowed Bar Harbor and its vicinity with a beauty as rare as it is wonderful. Lake and ocean, mountain and forest, extend their arms lovingly toward those who seek happiness in the realms of Nature and Nature's God. No fashionable element can destroy their beauty or dim their charms.

A man may be as much alone here as he could be in a "lodge in some vast wilderness," the solitude being the only idea in this simile that is applicable, for there is nothing akin to a wilderness on Mount Desert. He need not mingle in the whirl of gayety or be disturbed by its revelry. The solitudes of the mountain and glen are his; the old gray ocean has secrets for him which he does not share with the giddy throng, and the lake and stream are as pure and unsullied as when first the Indian paddled his birch bark canoe on its bosom or trapped the beaver by its banks.

Yes, there are various roads to happiness at Bar Harbor, and they are entirely independent of each other. The lover of Nature and the sportsman will be as much at home here as is the habitue of the ballroom; and the place is as free to one as to another.

WALKS.

For him who chooses to regard the visit to Bar Harbor as a "trip to the country" for rest and mild recreation, rather than as an opportunity to continue the social dissipation of the winter throughout the summer, we can open up a vast field for enjoyment. For him the summer days at Bar Harbor will be one uninterrupted round of health-giving pleasure and exercise, with nights of cool repose for which the enforced dweller in the city would almost barter his soul's salvation.

There are the LAKES, in all their virgin purity, smiling as sweetly in the sunlight as though they had never known the icy fetters of winter. He can launch his boat on one of them and pulling in under the shadow of the mountain peaks let go the anchor and give himself up to meditation. Here he can dream away the day in idle fancies, the silence unbroken save by the drum of the partridge calling to his mate, or the lazy splash of trout in pursuit of the heedless fly. If he is an angler he may drop his line in almost any lake with every chance of success. Then, after a day spent in this manner, what pleasure, as the evening shadows of the mountains touch the eastern shore, to wend his way homeward leisurely under the arching limbs of the forest trees to a repose sweetened by the unwonted exposure to the bracing air.

Then there are our WOODLAND WALKS. Not such as you can find any day on the outskirts of a town—a level road or side walk overshadowed by trees; those walks are tame. But here is one, such as no place outside of Mount Desert can boast of. It is the walk by the side of DUCK BROOK; and we give it as a sample of the numerous ones open to the visitor's selection.

You start in the early morning, long before the wearied dancers from last night's ball have even thought of rising; perhaps just as they may be going to bed. You pass out of the village by beautiful EDEN STREET; green meadows sloping on one hand toward a sun-kissed sea, on the other side rocky hills covered with foliage. On each side of you are numerous examples of what wealth and art can accomplish—handsome residences, homes of Bar Harbor's summer aristocracy. Gradually the towers on the hotels in the City by the Sea grow less in the distance, and at last you come (at about a mile distant from the village) to a merry brook, laughing and leaping down a leafy glen.

Leave the highway here and follow that brook. It may not lead you to "haunts of coot and hern," but you will find yourself in a fairy's paradise. Every mossy boulder you climb over, every leafy corner you turn, you expect to land in a bosky dell and find yourself the guest of Titania and her elves. Here, with a book in your hand, you can lie down under a shady tree and thus while the hours; or, wandering at your sweet will, with better company than yourself, you may pluck the wild flowers and crown your attendant nymph queen of your heart. If you are a reader you can have no better companion on these woodland rambles than Mrs. Burton Harrison's sweet little book, "Bar Harbor Days," or Mr. Hayes' "Jesuit's Ring," a thrilling romance of the French occupancy of Mount Desert. There are hundreds of spots like this Duck Brook glade, "far from the madding crowd's ignoble strife," where you may pass the summer days in rest and quiet, abandoning yourself to the enjoyment of a rural life.

Again there are the MOUNTAINS to climb, the views from the summits repaying one more than an hundred-fold for the healthy exertion necessary to reach them. A description of one of those MOUNTAIN WALKS will suffice to show the reader some of the pleasures attendant. Not that there is any sameness about Mount Desert mountains, for they each (seventeen in all) present a different panorama of scenery to the spectator; but that having enjoyed the visit to one mountain, the tourist will not give up till he has seen them all.

Let us storm NEWPORT MOUNTAIN, that tall and grim old sentinel who keeps watch so faithfully over the southern pass to this garden. The first part of the journey lies over the Schooner Head road, and may be accomplished either by driving or afoot. About one mile from the village you leave the main road, turning off to the right into a shady woodland path leading downward to a beautiful little pool of clear, cool water. This is just such a pool as the Naiads would have delighted in, and one can almost picture to himself as he gazes into its quiet depths, unruffled by the passing breezes which fan the tops of the surrounding trees, the presence of some tutelary wood nymph. Crossing this pool by some stepping stones at one extremity of it, you arrive at the base of the mountain.

From this point the path winds up through a heavy growth of trees for some distance and is quite distinct, the soil being worn away by the passing of many feet. As you slowly wend your way upward, you are enlivened by the merry chatter of the squirrels as they dart from tree to tree, and limb to limb, now disappearing from view and anon regarding you slyly with their bright, twinkling little eyes from some bough overhanging the path. Now and again the stillness is broken by the drumming of the partridge, sounding near and clear at first but gradually dying away, as it were, in the distance.

Gradually the wood becomes more open, until at last you emerge again into the sunlight amid a stunted growth of pines. Perhaps stunted is not a very correct expression to use with regard to those trees; they are dwarfs, but of fair proportions and similar in every way but size to their brethren of the forest. Here, as it lies for the most part over bare ledges, the path is not so clear: but it has been generously buoyed out by former pedestrians with piles of small rocks.

If you are not careful at this part of the ascent, you will miss your course and bring up on the brink of a ravine, its sides overgrown with a thick mass of foliage, at the bottom of which is a marshy pool. Here, not unlikely, you may start a deer or two, for this is a favorite lurking place for that royal game. Retracing your way carefully to avoid falling over the rocks you again pick up the buoys and follow a due south course. Now you are clear of the dwarf growth of pines, and at last have but one bare ledge between you and the summit.

The breeze at this altitude is fresh and cool. Now the GREEN MOUNTAIN HOUSE begins to peep out over the dome-like summit of DRY MOUNTAIN, and gradually the mountain peak itself follows. The ledges here bear the unmistakeable imprint of the Great Ice Age, being worn so smooth by glacial action that they are slippery and treacherous to the unwary foot. Great detached masses of flat rock rest on the sloping summit of the mountain, enough to pave all the streets of New York city. Now ahead of you looms up a heap of rocks, with a tall pole in the center. It is the summit of NEWPORT MOUNTAIN. There is a rush, a scramble, and you stand breathless but delighted, feeling it may be, for the moment, as Balboa when he first viewed the Pacific from his mountain elevation on the Isthmus of Panama.

GREEN MOUNTAIN is the highest elevation on the island, but the view from its summit is inferior to that from Newport. It seems as though one could almost jump into the Bay from the top of Newport. The islands dotted here and there over the waters

VIEW OF BAR HARBOR AND GREEN MOUNTAIN.

of FRENCHMAN'S BAY, form a beautiful panorama at one's very feet; while the low-lying land beyond SCHOODIC POINT, comprising DYER'S POINT, PETIT MENAN POINT and PETIT MENAN ISLAND and lighthouse, seems almost within hail. The formation of the mountain, descending abruptly in steep precipices on the east and west sides, favors this impression.

The view up Frenchman's Bay toward SORRENTO and the LAMOINE shore is very beautiful. The many vessels out on the Bay seem like white-winged birds as they flit out and in between the islands. The towering summit of Green Mountain shuts out the view of Somes Sound and the western part of the island, but by following the ridge of Newport to the southward you obtain a magnificent view of the southeastern shore with the CRANBERRY ISLES and BAKER'S ISLAND in the distance. Descending from the ridge to the eastern side, you reach the edge of the precipice which overhangs the SCHOONER HEAD ROAD. It was here some years ago that a terrible accident occurred and a young lady belonging to the village was killed by a fall over these rocks. On the southern end of the ridge, at a lower elevation, is a beautiful little pond, surrounded by wooded slopes and plentifully stocked with black bass.

If this last picture does not satisfy the reader that the MOUNTAIN WALKS are among the attractive features of this famous resort, then has the writer grievously failed in the discharge of his duty in this respect.

For those who appreciate the beauties of Nature and yet like to mingle with their fellowmen in the enjoyment of them, there is no more pleasing walk than the TOW PATH. This favorite promenade extends from the steamboat wharf southward along the shore of the Bay to Cromwell's Harbor. It is only a footpath; no carriages can pass. And it is well that it is so, for an innovation in the shape of a driveway would destroy the romantic beauty of the scene.

Let us look at it some lovely evening in July. The moon has just risen above the hills across the Bay, and sheds a broad band of silvery light over the waters which break in tiny waves at our feet. Ever and again, like some white-winged phantom, a sail boat crosses this wake of light, to vanish immediately in the gloom which seems so dark in contrast to its brightness. Shadowy objects flit to and fro on the dark bosom of the Bay, probably canoes freighted with loving couples enjoying the calm, sweet silence of the night.

Away off in the distance, to the south, shines the warning light in the tower of Egg Rock lighthouse, like a brilliant star on the horizon; while to the north are the many twinkling lights of the yacht fleet at anchor in the harbor. Before us looms a black mass rising out of the waves, the steep, bold cliffs of the BALD PORCUPINE. All is silence upon the water save now and again some light refrain from the boating parties, or the strange weird cry of the loon, like the shriek of some lost soul going out with the tide.

Ashore, where we are walking, life abounds. The path by the rocks is illumined here and there by streams of light from the windows of the cottages nestling among the trees; and strains of music, from the musicians within, fall upon our ears. This is a favorite walk with lovers, and we meet many in all stations of life from the cook and coachman to the dude from Rodick's and the season's belle. There is plenty of company here, and one never tires of watching the tide of humanity as it flows by. By daylight the beach is the resort of nurse maids and their charges gathering shells and pebbles and wading in the little pools left by the receding tide. Many beautiful cottages are built along this shore, and the well-kept grounds extend to the edge of the path. Here and there, among the trees, we come across pretty lawns on which tastefully dressed ladies and gentlemen are engaged in a tennis tournament. Everyone we meet seems bent on pleasure, and everyone seems to know that this is a good place to find it. And so say we.

DRIVING.

Driving is the favorite pastime in Bar Harbor and everyone indulges in it, from the millionaire cottager who rides out in state with his costly equipage, to the hotel guest who is contented with the more modest and distinctly local production, the buckboard. Everything is favorable for driving here. The roads are in capital order, and an intricate network of them overspreads the island taking in every place of interest and introducing the tourist to some of the grandest and most beautiful scenery on the coast of America.

The BUCKBOARD deserves particular mention, as being the vehicle best suited to the roads of the island. The first buckboard was rudely fashioned out of two pairs of wheels with a couple of planks stretched between them and seats nailed or tied on the planks. But it has developed wonderfully, and some of the buckboards of the present day are marvels of the builder's and painter's arts. Many of them are now shipped to all parts of the country for persons who have first seen the vehicle here. The gentle swaying motion of the board while travelling at full speed over the hilly roads is simply delightful; and no person who has ever ridden on one, wishes to use any other kind of vehicle during his stay. They are now built to carry any number of passengers from two to twelve, and the largest ones are drawn by four horses.

The stables in the village contain many fine specimens of horse flesh, and there is no danger of the traveler being furnished with a poor "rig" if he is at all careful. The livery men employ skillful drivers who are well acquainted with all the points of interest on the island and can impart all manner of interesting information to the passengers.

The town authorities issue a list of the drives with the fares for one or more passengers annexed, and this list is carefully revised each year. All drivers and liverymen are licensed, and any guilty of over charging will be fined or lose their license. This list, corrected for the present year, is printed on another page and will be found extremely useful for reference. It would be well for those starting out on a long drive to provide themselves with plenty of wraps, including waterproofs, as showers may come up very suddenly at times and the evenings are generally pleasantly cool. Limited space will only allow a description of a few of the principal drives; the others we will mention, or refer the reader to the printed list.

Perhaps the drive which affords the most extended view is that by the carriage road up Green Mountain. It requires a good stout team to make the ascent, although the road is not very steep. The Eagle Lake Road is followed for about a mile out of the village, and then you turn sharply to the left. For some distance the road leads through a beautiful forest of pine, spruce and birch. To your right, through the foliage, you catch occasional glimpses of Eagle Lake, far below; while ahead rises a delusive succession of peaks, each one, in turn seeming to be *the* peak.

At last the woods are past and the road comes out on the open ledge. What a magnificent scene bursts on the view! Beyond the silvery waters of Eagle Lake rises the rocky dome of Sargent's Mountain, 1350 feet above sea level, the sides covered with a heavy growth of pine and cedar. Spread out almost at your feet lies the northern portion of Mount Desert, level as compared with the rest of the island, but dotted here and there with picturesque hills clothed in living green and spots of silver where the lakes lie embowered in the surrounding foliage.

To the right, sparkling in the sunshine, stretch the beautiful waters of Frenchman's Bay; and beyond it, on the mainland, a seemingly endless chain of mountain peaks rise one above the other till they are lost in the blue haze. Katahdin, lifting its grand head toward the clouds, marks the limit of the view. To the westward over the spur of Sargent's Mountain you can see the head of Somes Sound with its pretty little village nestling among the trees; and away in the distance is a blue strip of water, a portion of Penobscot Bay.

At each turn in the road new beauties reveal themselves. Through the gap between Pemetic and Sargent's mountains appears a strip of ocean studded with islands as far as the eye can reach. Turning abruptly to the left, the eastern coast of the island comes in view. At your feet lies the village of Bar Harbor, and the Bay; and stretching out toward the opposite shore the beautiful Porcupines in their garb of emerald green. Little clusters of white buildings on the mainland mark the sites of the numerous budding summer resorts: Lamoine on its lovely peninsula, Sullivan at the head of its beautiful bay, Sorrento with its pretty little harbor shut in by picturesque islands, and Winter Harbor with its green shores and rocky headlands.

The ascent is very gradual and need not be hard on the horses, as the scenery is such that anyone having an eye to the beautiful will rest a score of times ere he reach the summit. On nearly the highest point stands the SUMMIT HOUSE, a substantial structure bolted fast to the ledge. You get an elegant meal there, take an observation from the tower through the telescope and see MOUNT DESERT ROCK twenty miles out on the ocean if it is a clear day, and then you are ready for the descent again. Many visitors stay at the hotel over night to see the sunrise, a most magnificent sight.

The descent is made much more rapidly than the ascent, the swinging motion of the buckboard coming into full play. The whole trip need not occupy over three hours, and no three hours spent elsewhere could be as productive of health and enjoyment.

The OCEAN DRIVE is one of the grandest shore roads on the island. Here the visitor has a remarkable ocean view. The road leads southward from the village, entering the woods at the SCHOONER HEAD ROAD, coming out again at Schooner Head where the passenger may stop off to view the famous SPOUTING HORN and ANEMONE CAVE, then on past GREAT HEAD and THUNDER CAVE to join the Otter Cliffs' road near the summer residence of Major Aulick Palmer. On one side of the road tower the PEAK OF OTTER and NEWPORT MOUNTAIN, the sides overgrown with noble forests of pine and spruce; while on the other is a grand battlement of cliffs. The rocky scenery along the shore is magnificent. In some places the road runs down close to the water's edge; in others it winds along the edge of a precipice, at the base of which, hundreds of feet below, the ocean is beating and throbbing continually. Nothing but sea meets the eye to the eastward; but what a sea! Nowhere in the world can the ocean present a more pleasing prospect under the rays of the summer sun, or a grander one when tempest-tossed.

The places of interest which may be visited on this drive besides those above stated are NEWPORT BEACH on the western side of Great Head; STAG CAVE so called from the fancied resem-

blance to that animal on its white quartz cliff; and a tall, battlemented cliff known as CASTLE HEAD. OTTER CLIFFS are well worth visiting, especially after a storm when the surf breaks grandly against them. The SPOUTING HORN does not spout unless after an easterly gale and at half flood tide, when the scene along the cliffs is magnificent.

This drive may be delightfully varied by keeping on to the right till the Otter Creek road is reached, and then driving home to Bar Harbor through the wild and picturesque scenery of the GORGE. This famous pass lies between the steep, bare cliffs of DRY MOUNTAIN and the more wooded precipices of NEWPORT. The road passes near the base of Newport, and between it and Dry Mountain is a meadow with a little brook rippling through it. The GORGE is one of the grandest pieces of scenery on the whole island. The round drive is only fifteen miles, and yet it takes in many of the most beautiful spots in the neighborhood of Bar Harbor.

The CORNICE ROAD is another beautiful shore drive. The tourist leaves Bar Harbor by way of Eden street, and after passing by the many handsome residences for which this road is justly celebrated and crossing a bridge over DUCK BROOK, he finds himself climbing a steep hill at the summit of which a glorious view of the Bay bursts upon him. This is the beginning of the CORNICE ROAD; and for nearly a mile and a half it winds along the steep side of a heavily-wooded hill, with overhanging rocks and trees on the one hand, and the beautiful waters of the Bay a hundred feet below on the other. Near its northwestern terminus the road turns a little inland, leaving room on the shore side for the handsome summer residences of J. Pierpont Edwards of New York, and John A. Morris one of the millionaire owners of Tuxedo Park and a Louisianian. Passing these houses the road crosses a small bridge over a brook, and, sweeping to the right, loses its identity in the highway which follows the northern shore of the island to MOUNT DESERT BRIDGE at the NARROWS. The first village on the county road is Hull's Cove, the former home of the De Gregoires, the old French family already mentioned in our history of the island. Crossing the Cove the road winds up a steep hill, passing on the right the pretty wooded promontory of POINT LEVI. Here are the cottages of Dr. Guy Fairfax Whiting of Washington, and C. Wycliff Yulee, son of the late Senator Yulee of Florida.

About three miles from Hull's Cove a road on the right leads down to the shore of the Bay and the visitor has an opportunity of viewing the OVENS, a number of caverns worn by the action of the sea out of the tall cliffs. There is a pretty beach here, and the Ovens can be visited at low water. A little further along the main road lies the village of SALISBURY COVE, and, beyond, EDEN and then the NARROWS. Instead of coming back the same way, the trip may be agreeably varied by going from MOUNT DESERT BRIDGE by the TOWN HILL road to the head of SOMES SOUND and thence home by EAGLE LAKE; or you may return as far as Salisbury Cove and take the NORWAY DRIVE, a beautiful wood road, through to the Eagle Lake Road.

The TWENTY-TWO MILE DRIVE is one of the pleasantest and most varied on the island. You take the Eagle Lake Road at the head of Mount Desert street. After passing Eagle Lake and the entrance to the BREAKNECK ROAD (a very misleading name, for the road is now in excellent order), the road crosses McFARLAND'S HILL from which a fine view can be had of BLUE HILL, UNION RIVER BAY and CAMDEN HILLS. Seven miles from Bar Harbor SOMES SOUND is reached, and then the road swings to the left following the eastern shore of the Sound, which is one of the most beautiful sheets of water on the coast and would make a harbor of refuge for the combined navies of the world. A mile from the head of the Sound is a beautiful pass between SARGENT and BROWN'S MOUNTAINS, the road being shaded by an avenue of beech, birch and maple. On the opposite shore are BEECH HILL and ROBINSON'S MOUNTAIN with ECHO LAKE in their vicinity. A little further along, the road passes between the ponds known as the upper and lower HADLOCK'S PONDS, and a mile further NORTHEAST HARBOR village comes in view. The road follows the east side of the harbor, passing several private residences, among them that of PRESIDENT ELIOT of HARVARD. Crossing the SEAWALL it runs through SEAL HARBOR village and then turns abruptly to the left. The road to JORDAN'S POND is left behind on the left and five miles further brings you to Otter Creek. Thence you may come home by the OCEAN DRIVE or through the GORGE.

For the SOMESVILLE DRIVE take the same route as on the Twenty-two mile drive to the head of the Sound. Cross the head of Somes' Harbor, whence a magnificent view of the SOUND is obtained. A little further along is the village of SOMESVILLE. Here you can take the road to Town Hill and thence, by Hull's Cove, back to Bar Harbor. The better way however is to take dinner at Somesville and devote the remainder of the day to BEECH HILL and ECHO LAKE. This drive might be pleasantly varied by starting from Bar Harbor early in the morning, visiting BEECH HILL in the forenoon and returning by way of Seal Harbor and the Ocean Drive.

To visit JORDAN'S POND you turn off the Twenty-two Mile drive a mile to the eastward of Seal Harbor at a sign board bearing the name of the Pond. A mile and a half brings you to the old JORDAN HOUSE at the southern end of the Lake. There is good accommodation here for man and beast. JORDAN'S POND is about two miles long by half a mile wide, and, except the southern end, is surrounded by mountains—PEMETIC on the east and a spur of SARGENT'S MOUNTAIN on the west, with the TWIN BUBBLES to the north like two giant sentries guarding the pass to EAGLE LAKE. There are boats here which can be hired on application at the farm house, and the pond is well stocked with trout. A road from the north end of Jordan's Pond leads across to Eagle Lake.

GREEN MOUNTAIN as we have already mentioned can be climbed by the carriage road. But it can also be visited by taking the barges of the GREEN MOUNTAIN RAILWAY Co., at the village, riding out to Eagle Lake, taking the steamer at the head of the lake for the base of the mountain, and then ascending by the railway to the summit. The railroad works on the same principle as the Mount Washington road, and visitors can ascend with perfect safety and have the benefit of the magnificent scenery during the climb.

From "Bar Harbor Days." Copyright, 1867, by Harper & Brothers.

A CANOE PARTY.

The description of the drives and places of interest might be prolonged indefinitely, for there is no lack of material; but it is unnecessary to weary the reader. The few specimens we have given will undoubtedly prepare him for some of the beauties which await him, though the description falls far short of the reality. In closing this section we would suggest that all those places may be visited on foot, and an adventurous pedestrian would find the trips full of pleasure and profit to him; but, still, he would miss the delightful sensation of the buckboard ride, a pleasure inseparable from and peculiar to Bar Harbor life.

BOATING.

FRENCHMAN'S Bay is one of the finest sheets of water for boating on the eastern coast of the United States, and visitors to Bar Harbor take due advantage of this fact. In summer its waters are dotted all over with crafts of every description, from the tiny bark canoe to the largest steam yacht. Many of the summer residents bring their yachts or boats with them; but no one will find any difficulty in getting any kind of craft he may fancy, at a very moderate charge for the hour, day or season.

The BOAT WHARVES are situated at the foot of MAIN STREET, within a few yards of the Maine Central wharf. They are three in number; and the proprietors, besides renting boats, have always a number of men on hand, one or more of whom will be sent with any party desiring their services. For those visitors who are not very familiar with the handling of a sail boat, it is always safest to have a "skipper," as sometimes, with the wind off the land, it is rather squally near shore. There are real Indians too who will take ladies out for a paddle in the canoes; a very pleasant experience, for those tiny birch bark craft ride the waves "like a thing of life," and, with an Indian at the paddle, will live in almost any kind of weather.

There are many points of interest in the Bay which can be reached in small boats or canoes. One may visit the OVENS in this way very pleasantly; and the opposite shores of the Bay are full of nooks and inlets where picnic parties may land and pass the day. The PORCUPINES, four rocky, wooded islands stretching in a chain across the Bay from Bar Island, are within easy sail or row of the wharves. They are all delightful spots for picnics, and on some of them are pretty grottos which can be reached at low tide. On LONG PORCUPINE, the furthest from the wharf, are a great many caves or clefts, extending from the top of the bluffs, over one hundred feet in height in some places, to the sea. Across one of these clefts is a picturesque natural bridge. A climb to the top of BALD PORCUPINE will give the adventurous pedestrian a delightful view of the Bay and the neighboring islands. On BURNT PORCUPINE is a large cavern, only accessible at low water, where a boating party nearly came to grief a few years ago, the lady and gentlemen composing it being forced to stay over night in its dark recesses. Another pleasant visit is to EGG ROCK and its lighthouse, which can be reached in an hour with a good breeze. On TURTLE ISLAND, on the Gouldsboro shore, is a good wharf and an excellent grove for picnics. The BAR HARBOR CANOE CLUB, with three hundred members, has a beautiful club house built out over the water on the northern shore of Bar Island, in which it holds receptions once a week during the height of the season; and its canoe parades are a pleasing feature of Bar Harbor life. A gentleman can take his lady canoeing along the shore, and when tired of the water they can land and indulge in the time-honored pastime of ROCKING, i. e. lounging among the rocks, with an umbrella or sunshade set to keep off inquisitive eyes, and reading aloud or flirting as they may elect.

The FISHING in the BAY is excellent. A good cat-boat or a small steam launch, either of which may be hired at the wharf, with hooks and lines and a bucket of clams, will give the tourist more sport than he ever expected to find on salt water. COD and HADDOCK abound, if you only know where to go for them, and an ordinary fisherman can fill his boat in half a day. There are good FISHING GROUNDS off EGG ROCK and SCHOONER HEAD, and further up the Bay above the Porcupines and at BALL ROCK. The boatmen at the wharf will tell you where to go, or accompany you if you desire it. Smelt, flounders and pollock can be caught off

the wharfs or from the lobster cars in the harbor; while the clam
and losbter *fishing* is all that can be desired.

Boating is a very general pastime at Bar Harbor. The harbor
is always full of yachts, the owners of which are continually taking their shore friends off for a cruise. There are more or less
boat and canoe races every year; and nearly every year Bar
Harbor is visited by some of the NORTH ATLANTIC SQUADRON,
when regattas and boat drills become the fashion. Pleasure
steamers are often hired by parties wishing to cruise along the
shores of the island or to visit some of the other resorts in the
vicinity. These parties are generally accompanied by bands of
music; and from June to September the Harbor and Bay present
a scene of festivity which is rarely equalled at any other place.

FISHING.

EAGLE LAKE, the Queen of Mount Desert's inland waters, is
situated at the base of Green Mountain, about two and one half
miles from Bar Harbor. All around it are grand mountain peaks,
while its pretty beaches are fringed with evergreen foliage. It
is this lake which gives Bar Harbor its water supply; and it is
here that the fisherman can find all the sport he desires and many
fine fish.

From time immemorial Eagle Lake has been the home of the
speckled TROUT, but it was not until 1886 that it was stocked with
twenty thousand salmon fry. Now these LAND-LOCKED SALMON
have grown to a weight of from four to six pounds, and are just
large enough and smart enough to give the angler a great deal of
fun and a good deal of work in catching them. From June, all
through the summer, they take the fly, live minnow or worm; and
no fisherman need come home without a good basketful. The
largest trout, of which there are great numbers, weigh four pounds,
and some have even been caught of five pounds weight.

There are two houses at the head of the lake, the EAGLE LAKE
HOUSE and the CURRAN HOUSE, where visitors can hire boats,
fishing tackle and guides, and where meals can be procured at any
time of the day. Mine Host of the Eagle Lake House has some

nice rooms which he will rent at a moderate price to those who wish to spend a few days near the scene of their sport; while both he and Landlord Curran are old and expert fishermen and can tell just where the big fish lie.

Great care has been taken lately of Eagle Lake. Its waters have been protected during the winter, and a fishway is being built this spring to allow the salmon to go back from the brook after spawning. It will be stocked each year with salmon fry, and

Mrs. R. B. Scott's Cottage, "Thirlstane," on Malden Hill.

grown fish are to be introduced into its waters from the hatching works at Reed's Pond. Smelts are put in the lake to feed the fish; and these, with the trout and salmon, are the only kind of fish in it. Everything is advantageous for the growth of the young fish; and, in a few years, it will be the leading lake in Maine for trout and salmon fishing.

Jordan's Pond is a great field for trout fishing; and a little pond among the hills in its neighborhood, known as Bubble Pond, is also full of them. Near Northeast Harbor, Hadlock's Ponds contain some of the prettiest trout on the island; while LONG POND, a large sheet of water near Somesville, and ECHO LAKE in the same district, are both plentifully stocked with the same delicious fish.

In the WITCH HOLLOW POND, near Duck Brook, black bass abound; and there is a small pond on the BREAKNECK ROAD, called HALF MOON POND, which is alive with black bass. Landlord Roberts of the Newport House and G. W. Dillingham of New York, own this pond, and will readily grant permission to any fisherman to try his luck there.

The TROUT STREAMS on the island are the brook in the GORGE MEADOW, one at HUNTER'S BEACH on the Seal Harbor road, and one on the NORWAY DRIVE, besides several other smaller ones. Bar Harbor is the fisherman's paradise without doubt.

In September the woods abound with partridges; and there is excellent plover shooting along the shores of the Bay. Woodcock are very plentiful on the line of the Maine Central railroad from Mt. Desert Ferry to Ellsworth; and there is rare sport in sea-bird shooting on the Bay later in the season.

SOCIETY LIFE.

When it is remembered that there are upwards of one hundred and fifty cottages at Bar Harbor, occupied during summer by their owners, the elite of society from Boston, New York, Philadelphia, Washington and others of our large cities, the visitor will be prepared for a great deal of gayety. . We know of no better way to picture the social life of the village than by giving a synopsis of the gayeties of last summer, with the names of a few of the society leaders.

The KEBO VALLEY CLUB HOUSE, a beautiful building erected in the midst of fine grounds near the Eagle Lake road, is the centre of amusement for the fashionables. In the building are a pretty little theatre and a restaurant; and the grounds include a race track, a baseball field and several lawn tennis and croquet lawns. Most of the ladies and gentlemen who visit Bar Harbor and form its summer society, belong to this club. The Club

House was formally opened the 18th of July, last year, on which occasion were present a large number of society's favorites, conspicuous among whom we find Hon. and Mrs. James G. Blaine and Senator and Mrs. Hale. During August the little theatre was the scene of a "Mother Goose" party originated by Mr. and Mrs. William F. Apthorpe of Boston, in which all the belles of the season took part. Then there was a reception given to President Harrison the same week; a representation of a burlesque of the opera L'Africaine, later, in which many of the leaders of society took part; tennis tournaments and horse races too num-

KEBO VALLEY CLUB HOUSE, EAGLE LAKE ROAD.

erous to mention; and a DRIVING PARADE in which Mrs. Burton Harrison, wife of the late Jefferson Davis' ex-private-secretary, took a leading part. This last was the affair of the season, and was after the style of the floral parades which have been given at Lenox and Newport. Promenade band concerts were given each day at the Club House, and the place was a constant scene of gayety.

Another of the flourishing clubs at Bar Harbor is the CANOE CLUB. This has a membership of over three hundred, with Mr. Edmund Pendleton as Commodore. At their pretty club house on Bar Island receptions are given every week during August and they have an annual parade which is a scene of gayety and festivity.

Then there is the Mount Desert Reading Room, a handsome structure near the wharf, with an elegant cafe and billiard-rooms, besides a library, drawing-rooms and large verandahs overlooking the Bay. Here many of the gentlemen pass most of their time in social chat or reading.

Besides all these there are the hops or Germans at the hotels every night during August; the annual tennis tournament at Mossley Hall, the home of W. B. Howard and family of Chicago; the receptions and dinners at the cottages; the parties on board the yachts and on the men-of-war which visit here regularly every year; the picnics; the sailing parties; the garden-parties; the yacht races; and, in fact, everything which helps to pass time and furnish pleasure for the gay and fashionable.

Last year, in addition to all these, there was a pretty fair at the Malvern Hotel in aid of St. Silvia's Catholic church; and a Kermesse at Rodick's for the benefit of the Village Improvement Association.

Add to all these the driving and visiting which people in this station of life keep up, and it will be evident to all that Bar Harbor in summer is one of the gayest places in the country.

It would be invidious to mention any of the names of the society people who visit here, unless we completed the list; but there can be no harm in detailing the celebrities.

Last year there visited Bar Harbor, President Harrison; Secretary Blaine, who has a cottage here; Secretary Tracy; ex-Secretary Whitney; Senator Hale; M. Roustan, the French Minister; Mavroyeni Bey, the Turkish Minister; Count Foresta, of the Italian Legation; Hon. Henry Cabot Lodge; Hon. Elijah A. Morse; Hon. John R. Thomas; Andrew Carnegie; Major Handy, and Private Secretary Halford; a goodly array of political and ministerial power; while a list of society stars from the different cities of the Union, who occupy cottages or pass the summer at the hotels, would take up many pages of this work.

The * Cottagers.
* * *

The valuation of the town of Eden (practically Bar Harbor) for 1889, amounted to nearly $5,700,000. Of this vast sum about $3,000,000 represented non-resident interests. Many of the wealthiest and most aristocratic people of Boston, New York, Philadelphia, Washington and other large cities of the Union have made themselves summer homes here; and the figures just given must convince the reader that they have not been niggardly in their outlay. In fact Bar Harbor can boast of more beautiful and costly residences than any other watering-place in America.

In Bar Harbor vernacular these residences are called "cottages," and the term is apt to mislead a stranger. On his first visit he will be likely to look around for those sylvan retreats which he has so often heard mentioned, expecting to find some little, one-story cottages embowered amid the woods on the hill side or nestling in some shady valley, only discoverable by stumbling across them accidently on some woodland walk. He will be totally unprepared for the handsome, stately piles of architecture which greet him at every turn. Bar Harbor "cottages" have cost their owners all the way from $10,000 to $100,000. Certainly "love in a cottage" of such a description would be a very pleasant state of affairs. It would be impossible in a work of this size to cite all the one hundred and fifty or more cottages in the village, so we must confine ourselves to the mention of a few of the more noteworthy.

EDEN STREET, with its branches, is essentially the street of cottages: in that vicinity they are about seventy-five in number. The pretty shore to the eastward is dotted along its entire length to Duck Brook with beautiful structures reflecting the taste and wealth of their owners. Here are the BARNACLES and BAGATELLE both the property of Edmund Pendleton, the author of "A Conventional Bohemian." A little further along is the SEA URCHINS, the summer home of Mrs. Burton Harrison, the charming author of "Bar Harbor Days." Secretary Whitney and his family occupied the cottage in 1887. Close to the road side is CLOVERCROFT, famous for the musicales given by its accomplished owner Mrs. George Place of New York. On the shore, near the

MRS. JOHN WHITAKER'S COTTAGE, "THE MOORINGS," ON EDEN STREET.

Harrison's cottage, is the residence of Rev. F. H. Johnston of Andover, called VILLA MARY. On the high ground to the left of Eden street, nearly opposite Miss Place's cottage, is STEEPWAYS, the summer home of the celebrated New York surgeon Dr. Wm. Tod Helmuth; and a little nearer the town is Prof. Geo. Harris' cottage. Further along and still higher up than Steepways, the magnificent architecture of MIZZENTOP, the home of Mrs. W. M. Hunt, the late Boston artist's widow, looks down on the road. Beyond the Sea Urchins, on the shore, is BEAUDESERT, the handsome residence of W. S. Gurnee the New York banker; and, beyond it, BURNMOUTH, W. P. Walley's home. Near Duck Brook are EDENFIELD, the beautiful cottage of the late Samuel E. Lyon of New York, and GUY'S CLIFF where E. C. Cushman, relative of Charlotte Cushman and a wealthy resident of Newport, resides. On the high ground opposite Edenfield stands GREYSTONE, the cottage of M. C. Lea the Philadelphia publisher.

The high ground on the western side of Eden street is opened up by two roads, CLEFTSTONE and HIGHBROOK, on which are situated some very handsome houses. On Highbrook road is STANWOOD, Secretary Blaine's beautiful cottage; and, near it, is MOSSLEY HALL, the home of the railroad magnate W. B. Howard of Chicago. On that part of this hill known as ABBY'S RETREAT, stand AVAMAYA the summer residence of Capt. Geo. M. Wheeler, Corps of Engineers, U. S. Army, and BAN-Y-BRYN, Mr. A. C. Barney's cottage.

KEBO STREET has some very beautiful cottages, almost all designed by De Grasse Fox of Philadelphia, and his property. Among these the DUTCH COTTAGE, so called, is a favorite. It was occupied last summer by Mrs. De Lancey Kane of Newport. The cottages of Morris K. Jesup of New York and Prof. E. W. Bass of West Point, are very handsome.

On the BAY SHORE, that section between the steamboat wharf and Cromwell's Harbor, are a number of elegant residences. Next the Club House is the little cottage built in the early days of Mount Desert by the late Alpheus Hardy of Boston, the pioneer cottager of Bar Harbor. The handsome granite house of later years stands back from the shore, in its rear. Beyond this is the residence of the Boston oculist, Dr. Hasket Derby. Following the shore along we pass EDGEMERE, the house of T. B. Musgrave of Wall street, New York, and come to DEVILSTONE, built by Mrs. Bowler, occupied one year by Wm. H. Vanderbilt, and now the property of J. T. Woodward of New York. Further along is the residence of the Boston millionaire, J. Montgomery Sears; and across Cromwell's Harbor, on Ogden's Point, is the present estate of Geo. W. Vanderbilt, which he has been improving the past year at an immense outlay. WATERSMEET, the cottage, and the estate were formerly the property of the late Gouverneur M. Ogden of New York, one of Bar Harbor's earliest cottagers.

The pretty cottage looking down on the village from the top of Strawberry Hill, is the summer residence of Dr. and Mrs. May of Washington. At BEAR BROOK, on the Schooner Head road, is the cottage of Mrs. Livingston, *nee* Bowler. On MALDEN HILL, overlooking Kebo street, is THIRLSTANE, the mansion of Mrs. R. B. Scott of Washington; and near it stands TOPPINGWOLD, Col. F. W. Lawrence's cottage. Lower down the hill INGLESIDE, Rev. Wm. Lawrence's cottage, appears.

These are only a few of the many beautiful residences in and near the village. Besides the non-residents' cottages, are about fifty cottages owned by natives and rented to visitors every year.

Piazza of "Stanwood," Hon. James G. Blaine's Bar Harbor Residence.

Cost * of * Living.

* * *

COTTAGE LIFE.

How much does it cost the visitor to live at Bar Harbor? In this and the following section we shall endeavor to answer that question. As far as cost is considered there are two distinct classes of visitors, the cottager and the hotel guest. The cottager, (and by this we mean the visitor who either occupies his own cottage or one which he leases, and keeps house in it) is the person to be spoken of in this chapter.

People about to spend their first season at Bar Harbor either in their own cottage or in one which they have rented, have very often thought it necessary to purchase their groceries and furnishings in the city and send them down here by the vessel load: they have never done it a second time. They labored under the grievous error of supposing this to be a little, one-horse, country village, with perhaps one or two general stores where the natives assembled to smoke their pipes and discuss politics and the weather. One summer's experience has shown them their mistake. They discovered that what they had paid out for freight on their supplies was just so much dead loss to them, and that they could get goods here of as fine a quality and at as cheap a rate as they could in the city. Besides this, in the matter of furniture, art goods, millinery and clothing, they found here branches of the houses which they had always dealt with at home, and they were even waited on by the same people who had already grown familiar with their tastes and had served them many times over the city counters.

And there are other articles which can be procured here much cheaper than they possibly can be in the city. Our marketmen have their own farms where they raise vegetables and force early delicacies for the table : and the milkmen have their dairys just out of the village, and supply the cottages every morning with much better milk, butter and eggs than can be had in the city. The famous creameries have agents in town also, and Darlington and other kinds of fancy butter can be always had at city prices.

There are a dozen groceries in the village, with as complete a stock of goods as any city shop can carry ; and they sell as cheap. Half-a-dozen markets cater to the cottage trade, and get their meats, fish and game from the most reliable sources. The early fruits and vegetables are here as soon as they are received in the cities. Delivery wagons go their rounds daily ; and affable, intelligent clerks attend to the wants of customers. The dry goods houses are second to none in the state ; the art goods, bric-a-brac and furnishing establishments, are branches of the most celebrated city houses. You can have your cottage built, and furnished from kitchen to attic in the most expensive and elegant style, without leaving the village. You can supply your table as well as you would that of your town house and at as cheap a rate. Ladies can procure the services of the best *modistes* and the most fashionable milliners, and gentlemen can have their wardrobes replenished and purchase lawn tennis and yachting costumes, just as they might at home. The boot and shoe shops carry as fine a line of goods as any town shop ; and the harness dealers can fit you as well as anywhere. If you are sick there are a dozen doctors of both schools who can minister to you (among them some of the most celebrated of city physicians and surgeons who make their summer home here) ; and there are good druggists to fill out their prescriptions.

All other businesses are well represented. Two florists cater to the wants of society. Elegant restaurants (which if not exactly equal to Delmonico's are patronized by his patrons and considered by them first-class) furnish the tables of the cottagers, provide waiters, cater at picnics and garden parties, and serve up private dinners in their own rooms. We have an excellent photographer ;

stationers who keep supplied with the best of everything in their line; booksellers and newspaper-dealers; jewellers who do fine watchmaking and repairing; and branches from city confectioners' establishments. A dozen finely equipped livery stables furnish vehicles of all kinds for the public, with excellent horses and competent drivers. Good boarding stables give accommodation to the horses of those visitors who may have no stables of their own. The driving rates (as will be seen from a glance at the list of drives on another page) are very moderate and far below city prices; and the visitor may be sure of getting a good rig. No jaded hacks or old car horses in the teams here.

The Bar Harbor Banking & Trust Co. has an office in Mount Desert Block, Main street; and the First National Bank of Bar Harbor does business in the Rodick Block, corner of Main and Cottage streets. There are four law offices in the village; and real estate brokers and insurance agents are numerous.

There are music and musical instrument shops; piano tuners can be hired who can do a good job; and orchestras or bands can be had for dances or garden parties. Other trades there are, too numerous to mention, but all doing their work and selling their produce as cheap as any of the same business in a city.

We would refer you to the advertisements in this book for further information regarding our merchants and their wares.

Now, if you wish an answer to the question at the beginning of this chapter, figure up what it costs you to live at home, per month, and multiply it by the number of months you intend to stay here. This will give you quite a margin on the right side; but of course you must make allowance for extras, such as driving, boating, and other pleasures and expenses of country life. Then, if you have to lease a cottage, it will cost you from $250 to $1000 per season according to the style of house you wish to live in. The cottages of the summer residents let at a still higher figure; and you may pay $3000 per season, if you wish to go in for style.

What we wish to impress upon people is, that THEY CAN LIVE AS CHEAPLY AND AS WELL AT BAR HARBOR AS THEY CAN ANYWHERE; and that taking into consideration the doctors' and medicine bills and other kindred expenses prevented by the health-giving qualities of the place, a summer spent at Bar Harbor is a financial investment which will repay the individual at least fifty per cent.

HOTELS.

That the HOTEL RATES are very reasonable as compared with those at other summer resorts, will be seen from the following list. Of course there are a few hotels which are frequented by the wealthiest and most fashionable visitors, where the prices may be considered by the average tourist rather high; but it must be remembered that there is a certain class of people who will not believe that a thing is good unless they pay a long price for it, and to this class these hotels cater, giving them however a good equivalent for their money. In the following list, anyone who is rich enough to spend a few weeks in the country during the summer will find some house whose prices will suit him. In explanation of the list we would say that the expression "Single Room" means a room and board for one person; "Double Room," a room and board for two. "Table Board" is the rate charged for those known in Bar Harbor as "Mealers," i. e. those living in a cottage or having rooms outside and boarding at a hotel. The "Accommodation" means the number of people who can be roomed comfortably in the hotel.

THE BELMONT, MOUNT DESERT STREET. Accommodation, 120. Single Rooms, $14 to $16; double, $24 to $26 per week. Private parlors, $75 per season. Table board $10 per week. Transients $2.50 per day. J. C. Manchester, proprietor.

BIRCH TREE INN, COTTAGE STREET. Accommodation, 40. Single rooms, $12 to $16; double, $21 per week. Table board $1 per day. Transients $2 per day. J. A. Rodick, proprietor.

BREWER HOTEL corner of WEST and MAIN STREETS. Transient house for commercial travelers. Accommodation, 25. Board and room $2 per day. L. O. Collins, proprietor.

HOTEL DES ISLE, DES ISLE AVENUE off Main street. Accommodation, 40. Single rooms, $10.50 to $15; double, $16 to $20 per week. Table board $10.50 per week. $2.50 per day. A. I. Saunders, proprietor.

GRAND CENTRAL, corner Main and Mount Desert streets. Board and room, $10 to $21 per week. R. Hamor & Sons, proprietors.

THE LOUISBURG, ATLANTIC AVENUE, off Main street. Single rooms, per week, $21 to $25, $28, $31.50 and $35. Double rooms, $50, $56, $60, $65 and $70, per week. Private parlors $20 and $25 per week in July; $35 per week in August alone; or $25 per week for the season. Table board, $17.50 per week. Transients from July 1st to September 1st, $5.00 per day; before or after that time $4.00 to $4.50 per day. Special rates by the season. Proprietor, Miss M. L. Balch, Boston, Mass.

LYNAM'S, MOUNT DESERT STREET. Single rooms, $14 to $16 per week; double rooms, $24 to $26 per week. Private parlors, $60 to $80 per season. Table board, $10 per week. J. S. Lynam, proprietor.

THE MALVERN, KEBO STREET. Accommodation, 125. For rates and other information apply to De Grasse Fox, proprietor.

THE MARLBOROUGH, MAIN STREET opposite Cottage street. Accommodation, 75. Single rooms, $14 to $18 per week; double, $24 to $28. Private parlors, $10 per week. Table board, $10 per week. Transients, $2.50 per day. Manager, S. N. Higgins.

The NEWPORT HOUSE, near MAINE CENTRAL WHARF. Accommodation, with cottages, 150. Single rooms, $14 to $18 per week; double, $24 to $28. Private parlors, $12 per week. Table board, $1.25 per day. Transients, $2.50 per day. Proprietor, W. M. Roberts.

PARKER COTTAGES, MOUNT DESERT STREET. Apartment houses; rooms only. Bedrooms, $35 to $65 per season of three months. Parlors, $65 per season. E. C. Parker, proprietor.

The PORCUPINE, MAIN STREET, on the European plan. For information apply to F. P. Wood, Bangor.

The ROCKAWAY, near MAINE CENTRAL WHARF. Rooms only. Accommodation, 100.

The RODICK, MAIN STREET. D. Rodick & Sons, Proprietors.

ST. SAUVEUR and ANNEX, MOUNT DESERT STREET. Accommodation, 200. Single rooms, $16 to $21 per week; double, $30 to $38. Private parlors, $15 to $20 per week. Table board, $12 per week. Transients, $3.50 per day. Proprietors, Alley Bros.

The WEST END, WEST STREET, near Roderick street. Accommodation, 400. Single rooms, $15 to $25; double, $30 to $42. Table board, $10.50 per week. Transients, $3 to $4 per day. Parlors and baths extra. O. M. Shaw & Son, proprietors.

At nearly all of the above hotels, a reduction is made in favor of young children and servants; and, in general, some allowance is made in the case of large families.

Besides the hotels, there are several boarding-houses where board can be had at from $4 to $7 per week; and rooms can be rented in many of the blocks and residents' cottages at reasonable rates.

Routes to Bar Harbor.

* * *

The visitor to Bar Harbor may reach his destination by a variety of routes, and by rail or steamboat as he may select. Each has its peculiar attractions. We propose, in this chapter, to describe these routes, and then to give an approximate table of the cost of travel from many of the principal cities in the United States. The traveler comes as far as Boston by rail, and at that point the routes diverge.

The MAINE CENTRAL R. R. takes the passenger by the Boston & Maine R. R. from Boston, at Portland, and brings him down over its lines, through a beautiful stretch of country, to MOUNT DESERT FERRY, eight miles from Bar Harbor, where he steps on board the elegant steamer Sappho and is ferried across the lovely waters of Frenchman's Bay to his destination. During the summer season three trains per day, each way, are run over the Maine Central. They arrive about 8.30 A. M. and 6.00 and 7.30 P. M.; and leave at 5.00 and 10.30 A. M. and 4.15 P. M. There are Pullman sleepers on the morning train in and the afternoon train out; and parlor and dining cars on the others. The Mount Desert trains have the most elegantly equipped cars in the country; and the ride from Boston to Mt. Desert Ferry is a delightful pleasure trip. This season through Wagner cars will be run from Chicago via the Michigan Central to Niagara Falls, thence over the famous mountain line of the Maine Central through the White Mountains to Bar Harbor. There will also probably be Canadian Pacific sleepers from Chicago via the Wabash R. R. to Detroit and thence over the Canadian Pacific by way of Montreal.

Wagner drawing-room cars from Chicago, per chair $5.50. Parlor car to or from Boston, per chair $1.50; sleeper, per night, single berth $2.00, section $4.00, drawing-room compartment $7.00. Boston to New York: sleeper, per berth, $1.50; parlor car, per chair, $1.00. Boston to Philadelphia: sleeper, per berth, $2.00. Boston to Washington and Baltimore: sleeper, per berth, $2.50. Dining cars, $1 per meal.

The MAINE CENTRAL R. R. Co.'s steamer, CITY OF RICHMOND, leaves Portland, Me., every Tuesday and Friday at 11 P. M. or on the arrival of Pullman Express Train leaving Boston at 7 P. M., and touches at Rockland, Castine, Deer Isle, Sedgwick, Southwest Harbor and Northeast Harbor, arriving at Bar Harbor at 1 P. M. She goes east as far as Machiasport; and, returning, leaves Bar Harbor every Monday and Thursday at 10 A. M., arriving in Portland at 1 o'clock the next morning. Fare from Portland, $4.00. From Boston, $5.50. Staterooms, $1.00 and $1.50.

The BOSTON & BANGOR STEAMSHIP COMPANY's steamers leave Boston daily, except Sunday, at 5 P. M., connecting at Rockland, Me., next morning, with the STEAMER MOUNT DESERT which arrives at Bar Harbor about 10 A. M. Returning, leaves Bar Harbor daily, except Sunday, at 1 P. M. for Rockland and Boston. The Boston steamers are large sea-going, side-wheel vessels, with spacious saloons and elegant staterooms. There are about 100 staterooms on each steamer. The cuisine is excellent. Fare, $4.00. Return ticket, $7.50. Staterooms, $1.50 and $2.00.

The PLANT INVESTMENT COMPANY's elegant OCEAN STEAMER OLIVETTE, which during the winter carries the U. S. and West India Fast Mail between Port Tampa, Key West and Havana, runs between Boston and Bar Harbor direct. She leaves each port three times per week during the season, sailing from Boston about 6 P. M. and arriving at Bar Harbor in time for breakfast, leaving again the same evening. She is a very fast steamer, and is handsomely fitted up for the passenger trade with elegant staterooms and spacious saloons. Fare, $5.00. Staterooms, $2.00 to $4.00.

The handsome steamship, "Winthrop," has lately been purchased by the New York, Maine and New Brunswick Steamship Co., and will be put on the route between New York and Bar Harbor, direct. From Bar Harbor she will go to Eastport and St. John, N. B.

APPROXIMATE TABLE OF FARES.

First-class Limited Tickets—Per Rail.

San Francisco and Pacific Coast Points,	to Boston,		$92 50
New Orleans, La.,	"	"	38 00
Minneapolis, Minn.,	"	"	31 00
St. Paul, Minn.,	"	"	31 00
St. Louis, Mo.,	"	"	26 25
Chicago, Ill.,	"	"	22 00
Cincinnati, O.,	"	"	20 00
Cleveland, O.,	"	"	15 00

Note. Add $6.50 to above, for fare to Bar Harbor per rail.

Washington, D. C.,	to Boston,		12 25
Baltimore, Md.,	"	"	11 05
Buffalo, N. Y.,	"	"	10 65
Philadelphia, Pa.,	"	"	8 25
New York,	"	"	5 00
" " (by steamer)	"	"	4 00
Albany, N. Y.,	"	"	4 50
Saratoga, N. Y.,	"	"	5 15
Lenox, Mass.,	"	"	3 65
New Haven, Conn.,	"	"	3 40
Hartford, Conn.,	"	"	2 75
Narragansett Pier, R. I.,	"	"	2 35
Springfield, Mass.,	"	"	2 25
Newport, R. I.,	"	"	1 70
Providence, R. I.,	"	"	1 00

Note. Add $7.00 to above, for fare to Bar Harbor by rail.
For through rate per steamer Olivette add $5.00 to fare to Boston.
For through rate per Boston & Bangor steamers add $4.00 to fare to Boston.

Per Rail.

Toronto, Canada	to Bar Harbor,			$15 00
Quebec, "	"	"	"	13 50
Montreal, "	"	"	"	12 50
Halifax, N. S.,	"	"	"	11 00
St. John, N. B.,	"	"	"	6 50
Burlington, Vt.,	"	"	"	12 00
Poland Springs, Me.,	"	"	"	6 60

Congregational Church.

═Churches.═

✻ ✻ ✻

Bar Harbor might almost be called the "Village of Churches," for, small as it is, it contains no less than six sacred edifices. Of these but four are open all the year round, the Baptist, Congregational, Episcopal and Methodist; the Roman Catholic and the Unitarian are summer places of worship.

THE BAPTIST CHURCH on LEDGE LAWN AVENUE is a handsome wooden structure built in 1887. It has a tall tower at its southwestern corner, with the main entrance in its base. In the front is the vestry room, and above this a parlor which is used for church sociables. The main body of the church will seat about three hundred people comfortably. The windows are of stained glass. In the eastern end of the auditorium is an arched recess in which the pulpit stands; and to the left is the choir loft. The partition separating the vestry from the body of the church is made of panel-work in sections, and so hung with cords and weights that it can be slid up into the walls above, making the whole floor into one large auditorium. The interior finish is very handsome. The pews are of ash and the floor is carpeted. The whole floor, when the partition is raised, will accommodate about five hundred people. Rev. A. F. Palmer is the pastor of the church.

ST. SILVIA'S ROMAN CATHOLIC CHURCH is situated on KEBO STREET, in the midst of beautiful trees and in the neighborhood of many handsome cottages. It is a pretty wooden edifice and corresponds well with its surroundings. The building has a seating capacity of nearly five hundred. The pews are of ash, handsomely finished with black walnut. The altar is a magnificent piece of workmanship, delicately carved and tastefully decorated. It has three niches, the center one containing a beautiful cross carved by Joseph Mayr of Oberammergau, the man who took the role of Christus in the Passion Play at that village. The cross was a gift from Dr. Derby, one of the summer cottagers, to the church. The altar is flanked by beautiful stained windows with doves as centre pieces. This church is only open during the summer season, when the Rev. T. F. Butler of Ellsworth offici-

ST. SILVIA, CATHOLIC CHURCH, KEBO STREET.

ates. Several distinguished Roman Catholic clergymen visited the village last season and took part in the services; among them Archbishop Ryan.

The CONGREGATIONAL CHURCH is situated on MOUNT DESERT STREET nearly opposite the head of School street. Until 1888 its site was occupied by the old "White Church," a union meeting house and the first built in the town of Eden. The present building is of the Old English Gothic style of architecture, and was designed by W. R. Emerson of Boston. It is built of the native red granite, is cruciform and has a massive stone tower, with battlemented top and a sharp, shingled spire, on the southwestern corner. On the street front is a heavy granite porch, with two large handsome arches supported by buttresses with carved caps. This forms the main entrance to the church. The interior is lighted by a number of memorial windows. The rafters and trusses are finished in old oak, and the sheathing is of cherry. The arches spring from handsomely carved cluster-columns; and the wainscotting is of ash in elaborate designs. The birch floor is carpeted in the aisles; and the pews are of ash and handsomely upholstered. The pulpit and choir loft are in arched recesses in the northern end of the church. On the northeastern corner is a chapel or lecture-room, finished in elegant style and connected with the main church. The latter will accommodate about four hundred and sixty worshippers; the chapel has a seating capacity of one hundred and twenty-five. The church was 'dedicated last summer. Rev. Joseph Torrey, the pastor, is assisted during the summer by the visiting clergymen.

The EPISCOPAL CHURCH of ST. SAVIOUR is situated on the north side of Mount Desert street, a few rods west of the Congregational church. Between them lies the village churchyard. St. Saviour's, when first built in 1879, was a small church capable of seating about two hundred people. The present edifice was erected a few years ago. It is cruciform, and its walls are of red, untrimmed island granite finished in the rough both inside and out. In the center rises a large, square tower with hip-roof surmounted by a cross. The rafters and all the interior woodwork are stained a rich brown, forming a pleasing contrast with the lighter tint of the masonry. The handsome Italian-marble altar was donated by Mrs. Ogden of New York, in memory of her husband the late Gouverneur Morris Ogden, a vestryman of Old Trinity, New York city, and the treasurer of the committee in charge of St. Saviour's. Mr. Ogden's remains are buried under a brass plate in the nave of the church. There are several handsome memorial windows in the chancel and transept, presented by some of the summer visitors; and Mrs. W. H. Vanderbilt and Mr. J. Montgomery Sears have been gen-erous donors. St. Saviour's will accommodate about eight hundred worshippers. It has a fine organ; and the choir singing in summer especially, is excellent. There are five services each Sunday during the summer, at which a great many visiting clergymen officiate. Rev. Christopher S. Leffingwell has been rector of St. Saviour's since its institution. Connected with the church is a large chapel just recently completed, in which the Sunday school will be held in future.

The METHODIST CHURCH, on SCHOOL STREET, is a handsome brick edifice built in 1888. It is slate roofed, and has a square tower, ninety-six feet in height, on its northeastern corner. The main entrance to the church is in the base of this tower. On the street front is the lecture room which will accommodate about two hundred people. This room is connected with the main church by large folding doors, which when folded back practically throw the two rooms into one. The main body of the church is sixty feet square and will seat about four hundred people. In the western end is a semi-circular platform on which the pulpit stands, and behind this is the organ and choir loft. The ceiling is beautifully finished, the spaces between the exposed rafters being ceiled with matched pine. The wood work is all light colored; and light tinted plaster walls give a bright and cheerful tone to the interior. The large memorial windows of colored cathedral glass, are very handsome. The seating accommodation consists of assembly chairs arranged in nearly semi-circular rows, with receptacles for books, hats and umbrellas. A pretty woolen carpet covers the floor. The church is a notable addition to the many architectural triumphs in the village. Rev. G. G. Winslow is pastor.

The UNITARIAN CHURCH on LEDGE LAWN Avenue was built last year. It is a quaint but pretty little wooden edifice, with a two-storied tower, surmounted by a bell-shaped dome, on one corner. The extension of the hip-roof is supported by massive granite posts, and covers a driveway fourteen feet wide extending along the front of the building. Along one side of this driveway is a raised platform from which three large double doors, with wrought iron hinges, lead to the body of the church. The building is lighted by six windows, three on the north and three on the south. It has a seating capacity of two hundred and fifty. The plaster of the walls and ceiling is tinted in water color, and the wainscot consists of diagonal sheathing. In the ell are the organ and choir loft, and the pulpit and pastor's room. The ceiling is arched on the north and south sides, and the plaster work is panelled. The church was closed during the past winter; but last summer many distinguished preachers occupied the pulpit, among whom were the following: Revs. Edward Everett Hale, Charles Carol Everett, Brooke Herford, Samuel Longfellow and Francis Peabody, the latter one of our summer cottagers.

THE UNITARIAN CHURCH, ON LEDGE LAWN AVENUE.

METHODIST CHURCH, ON SCHOOL STREET.

Public ⊛ Conveniences.

✳ ✳ ✳

The village of Bar Harbor is illuminated with the ELECTRIC LIGHT. Fifteen powerful arc lights are set on high poles distributed through the principal streets. The shops, hotels and churches are lighted with the incandescent light, and many of the houses are also furnished with them. The company which controls the plant, will wire any cottage to order and supply the lights at reasonable rates. During the summer season the arc streetlights burn till one in the morning, and the incandescent lights are kept going till daylight. The Electric Light Station is situated on Edgewood street between Main and School streets.

The POST OFFICE is located on the north side of COTTAGE STREET, near Main street. Bar Harbor office belongs to the third class of post offices, and a bill has been introduced in Congress by the Hon. Seth Milliken for an appropriation wherewith to erect a government building here. Last Congress a bill for the same purpose was vetoed by President Cleveland. When the number of patrons during the summer is considered it would seem as though the Government ought to do something in that way. The present office is provided with about four hundred lock-boxes and one hundred and fifty call-boxes. The mail service during the summer is excellent, comprising three general mails per day each way, and several local distributions. The office does both DOMESTIC and FOREIGN MONEY ORDER business, and of course REGISTRY business. An iron LETTER BOX is placed on the steamboat wharf, where letters will be collected until five minutes from train time. Tables of arrival and departure of mails will be found in the local papers.

The WESTERN UNION TELEGRAPH CO. has an office on Main near the corner of Cottage street, which offers all the facilities of the usual telegraph office. The HANCOCK COUNTY TELEPHONE COMPANY has its central office at Room 20, Mount Desert Block, Main street, and branches in all the principal towns in the county. It also exchanges with Bangor, Belfast and Rockland, Maine.

The AMERICAN EXPRESS and the UNITED STATES EXPRESS companies, have offices within a few yards of each other on the west side of Main below Cottage street. They have express messengers on nearly all the boats and trains during the summer. There are always plenty of TRUCKMEN at the wharf on the arrival of the boats; and the hotels and livery-stables have their teams in waiting also.

For the better protection of the harbor Congress lately voted $80,000 as the nucleus of an appropriation large enough to build a BREAKWATER from the BALD PORCUPINE to a point inshore near the mouth of CROMWELL'S HARBOR. Work was begun on the structure in the spring of 1889; and the portion between the Porcupine and a ledge a third of the distance to the shore, was completed to low-water mark. The failure of the contractor put an end to the work last fall, for a time; but it is expected that it will be resumed this year. The structure will probably cost $5,000,000; but when finished it will make this one of the finest harbors on the coast.

The PUBLIC LIBRARY is situated on the corner of MOUNT DESERT and SCHOOL STREETS. It is open every day except Sunday during the season, both forenoon and afternoon. The library contains nearly five thousand volumes, selected with great care by the committee. A small fee is required from those taking books out, for the purpose of paying running expenses and keeping the books in repair.

Sewerage, Fire and Water Systems.

* * *

Beautiful Eagle Lake, at an elevation of two hundred and eighty feet above sea level, furnishes Bar Harbor with a supply of delightfully pure and cool water for domestic and municipal purposes. In every street are laid immense mains, and every house and hotel is piped in connection with them. Even in the hottest day in summer if the water be allowed to run a few minutes, it can be used as a beverage without the addition of ice: for those, however, who prefer "ice in theirs," there are companies with their delivery wagons ready to supply the native material at reasonable rates. On all the principal streets hydrants are set at regular intervals of a few rods, which will play a powerful stream in case of fire. All the hotels are protected in this manner. During the summer season street sprinklers are in constant use to lay the dust and cool the atmosphere; and drinking troughs for horses are set along the roads on the island.

The village has an excellent FIRE DEPARTMENT, with steam fire engine, two hose companies and a hook and ladder company; and the men are well trained to their business. A heavy fire-bell, in the Engine House near the Rodick, gives warning in cases of fire. The village has been singularly fortunate in regard to fires, only two of any consequence having occurred since Bar Harbor became a summer resort; and these fires were each confined to a single building. Watchmen patrol the streets at night; and all the hotels have their own private watchmen besides. What few fires have started besides the two just mentioned, have been ably handled by the fire brigade, even in cases exceptionably favorable to the spreading of the flames.

The SEWERAGE SYSTEM of Bar Harbor cost the town in the neighborhood of $120,000; but it is well worth the money expended. It was built from plans made by Ernest W. Bowditch, C. E. of Boston, and under his direct supervision. The entire sewage of Bar Harbor is emptied well out in the Bay, at a point far south of the village. On every street are mains, from one to two feet in diameter, laid in some places at a depth of twenty-four feet below the surface in the solid ledge; and every part of the immense network of pipes is far below the line of frost. Brick man-holes with iron covers, at regular intervals, allow of flushing the mains from the hydrants; and this is done frequently. Engineering experts say that Bar Harbor has the finest drainage system of any place outside of the largest cities; and certain it is that since its completion nothing in the nature of an epidemic has been known, and the general health of the town has been excellent. Taken in conjunction with the naturally healthy climate of the island, these sanitary arrangements make Bar Harbor the finest health resort in the United States.

A Few Words to Intending Visitors.

* * *

When you have decided to come to Bar Harbor and have engaged your rooms, the next thing is to consider your wants while here.

If you are to stay any length of time you will do well to bring a few articles with which to decorate your rooms and add to your comfort. These should generally be selected from what you already own, and not be purchased specially, for plenty of suitable things can be bought at Bar Harbor, and at full as low a cost when it is remembered that you can select to better advantage after seeing your rooms and taking time to consider their needs.

The storekeepers at Bar Harbor order in large quantities, at a minimum for freight, and do not ask a large profit, at the same time selecting goods suitable to the place and climate. There are also to be found here branches of city stores with large stocks to draw from.

Enterprising newsmen hurry the city papers along, and during the last season the New York and Boston Sunday papers were delivered to their patrons at least twelve hours ahead of the regular mail service.

If you are in a hurry to see your daily papers you should wait and order of a Bar Harbor newsman; if not, then order your paper direct from the publishers.

Books for seaside reading are now published in paper covers at so low a price that it will hardly pay to encumber your trunks with many; a few in your satchel for reading en route will be enough, and you can buy the new ones as they come out.

In the matter of perishable articles, fruits, and the like, you can buy finer qualities at Bar Harbor than is usual in the large cities, and the reason is that the dealers in these summer resorts are always ready to pay the highest prices as they have a market for fine goods, while the city dealer loses his best trade during the summer for his customers are all out of town.

Therefore do not overburden yourself with articles that can be bought here, and do not place orders for things to be sent you until you have seen what Bar Harbor can do for you and you will be better satisfied in the end.

I wish to announce that I have completed arrangements with Bailey, of West St., Boston, the celebrated confectioner (who has re-opened at his old place), for a full supply of his candies, fresh and pure. Also that I intend to make a specialty of his cocoanut cakes.

ALBERT W. BEE.

I shall keep on hand during the summer a good line of the best fruits, California, Southern and Eastern. These will be carefully selected, free from decay, and of a uniform size for each grade,—not little ones at the bottom—big on top.

ALBERT W. BEE.

As Lawn Tennis is one of the most popular out-door games at Bar Harbor, I have arranged for the agency of Wright & Ditson for their extensive line of sporting goods, and will furnish anything of their make at their catalogue prices, delivered at Bar Harbor. Their Tennis balls are the best.

ALBERT W. BEE.

I shall have as usual the finest line of Imported and Domestic Cigars, and will sell by the box at very little over the city prices. As I get cigars every few days they are fresh and not affected by the climate.

I also keep an extensive line of Tobacco and Cigarettes, including the Turkish and Egyptian.

ALBERT W. BEE.

All the leading newspapers for sale or ordered. Periodicals and Magazines at earliest date of publication. Special arrangements to insure early delivery of papers.

Orders taken for any length of time from one day to the season, and papers delivered anywhere in the village or at Northeast Harbor, or Southwest Harbor.

Don't order your paper from the publisher as I can give it to you one or two hours earlier than you could get it by mail.

ALBERT W. BEE.

MAINE CENTRAL RAILROAD,
THE RENOWNED ⋈
⋈ VACATION LINE.

The Great Highway of Travel in Northern New England,

With 664 miles of steel rails, reaching all the leading business centres of Maine, New Hampshire and Vermont, together with the eastern provinces of Canada; and also furnishing

RAPID TRANSPORTATION AND SPLENDID ACCOMMODATIONS. To and from a vast number of famous summer resorts and quiet resting retreats along the coast and interior of Maine and New Brunswick, forming the only all rail line to

BAR HARBOR
And the only route to the
WHITE MOUNTAINS,

Through the Celebrated Crawford Notch and connecting this great galaxy of famous summering places:

MONTREAL, NIAGARA FALLS, NORTH CONWAY,
QUEBEC, BETHLEHEM, SEBAGO LAKE,
THE GREEN MOUNTAINS, PROFILE HOUSE, PORTLAND,
LAKE CHAMPLAIN, WHITEFIELD, CASCO BAY,
BURLINGTON, JEFFERSON, OLD ORCHARD,
SARATOGA, AUSABLE CHASM, FABYANS,
RANGELEY LAKES, POLAND MINERAL SPRINGS,
CRAWFORDS, BOOTHBAY, MOOSEHEAD LAKE, ST. ANDREWS AND ST. JOHN.

ALSO OPERATING THE
PORTLAND, MT. DESERT & MACHIAS STEAMBOAT CO.,

Between Boston, Portland, and all points on the coast of Maine.

ARTHUR SEWALL.   PAYSON TUCKER,
President.   V. P. and Gen. Manager.

F. E. BOOTHBY, G. P. & T. A.

The attention of intending visitors to Bar Harbor is invited to the Steamship Service between

—BOSTON AND BAR HARBOR,—
AS PERFORMED BY THE
STEAMSHIP "OLIVETTE"
OF THE PLANT STEAMSHIP LINE.

The "Olivette" leaves Boston every Tuesday, Thursday and Saturday, at 6 P. M., and arrives at Bar Harbor the following morning at 7. Returning, leaves Bar Harbor every Monday, Wednesday and Friday, at 6 P. M. The fare by this line is, first-class, one way, $5.00, excursion, $9.00; second class, $3.00. State-rooms, $2, $3 and $4, according to size. The smaller state-rooms will accommodate two persons, while the larger rooms will accommodate three or four persons traveling together.

The steamship "Olivette" and the service performed on the above route have proven very popular with the visitors at Bar Harbor. Leaving Boston at six in the evening, viewing the Harbor and beautiful Bay of Boston, with its many interesting and historical points, by daylight, and after a pleasant night's sail reaching Bar Harbor the following morning, are the elements which have firmly fixed the popularity of the trip and the steamship by means of which it is accomplished. Built especially for passenger service and combining all the latest devices and improvements for safety, speed and comfort, large airy state rooms with incandescent lights; sumptuously furnished saloons and dining room, with unexceptionable meals—(table d' hote,) this steamship offers all the conveniences and comforts of a first-class hotel.

Through tickets are on sale and through baggage checks are provided at all principal points so that the journey to and from Bar Harbor may be made with the least trouble and with the least expense.

N. B.—The sailing time of the "Olivette" may at any time be changed upon due notice of same being given by the company.

LYNAM'S,
MOUNT DESERT STREET,
Bar Harbor, : : Maine.

PLEASANTLY SITUATED ON THE PLEASANTEST STREET IN BAR HARBOR.

Water View from rear and front of Hotel.

Beautiful Mountain View.

Well appointed in every respect.

Open from June until October.

Terms $12 to $16 per week.   Correspondence solicited.

J. S. LYNAM, Proprietor.

St. Sauveur Hotel,

ALLEY BROS., PROPRIETORS,

MT. DESERT ST., BAR HARBOR.

THE LOCATION OF THIS HOTEL IS ONE OF THE VERY BEST IN TOWN.

Unobstructed View
—— OF THE ——
MOUNTAINS AND OCEAN.

LARGE APARTMENT HOUSE
Connected with the Hotel.

Open During the Season.

Rates and other information will be furnished by
ALLEY BROS., Managers.

PORCUPINE ✷ HOTEL
—AND—
◁ CAFE. ▷

AMERICAN OR EUROPEAN PLAN.
Elegant In All Its Appointments.

ELEVATOR, ELECTRIC LIGHTS AND BELLS, BATH ROOMS, ETC.
ROOMS SINGLE AND EN SUITE,

PRICES REASONABLE.

THE ONLY HOTEL ON EUROPEAN PLAN AT A WATERING PLACE IN THIS COUNTRY.

THE FINEST SITUATION IN BAR HARBOR; VERY CENTRAL.

The Table d' hote at 6 P. M. is a Specialty.

The Cuisine and Service will retain the same excellence as in the past.

For particulars write to

FRANK P. WOOD.

The Belmont,

J. C. MANCHESTER,   Proprietor.

Bar Harbor, Maine.

* * *

Beautifully Situated on Mount Desert Street, the Most Fashionable Boulevard in Bar Harbor.

* * *

THE BELMONT HAS

Electric Bells,—

—Electric Lights

——and——

All Modern Conveniences.

* * *

HANDSOMELY APPOINTED,
LARGE MUSIC ROOM,
BEAUTIFUL LAWN,
PUBLIC TENNIS COURTS,
PRIVATE PARLORS.

Open from May 1st to Nov. 1st.

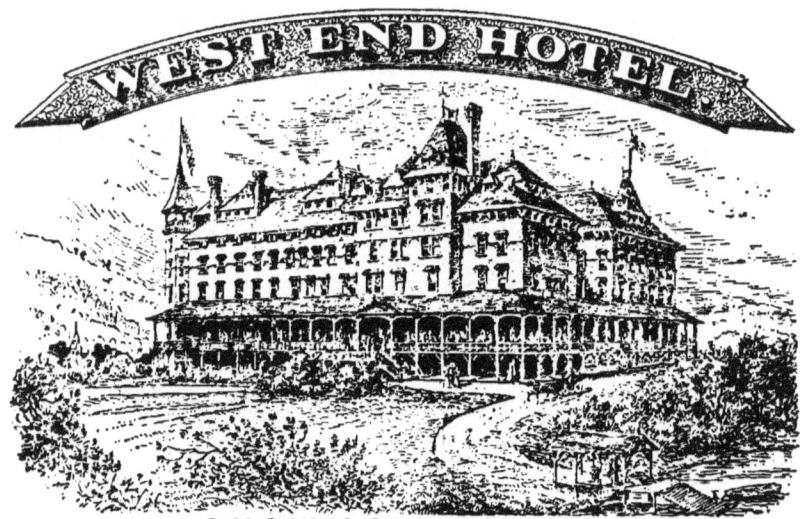

O·M·SHAW·&·SON,· PROPRIETORS·

This hotel is one of the largest and most modern hotels at Bar Harbor, and surpasses them all in its location, only three minutes' walk from the wharf, overlooking the harbor, Frenchman's Bay, and a beautiful view of the mountains, and of many of the finest cottages. The Cottage street entrance has much improved the hotel.

It has accommodations for four hundred guests, with all modern improvements, perfect drainage, electric lights, electric bells, gas, elevator, baths, steam heat, steam laundry, fire alarm, fire escapes, etc. The hotel has undergone extensive interior decorations since last season, and has now the finest specimens of Moresque decoration of any Hotel in America. The appointments, cuisine and service of this hotel are second to none, and no pains will be spared to make it first in all respects.

Rooms can be had in suites, with or without baths or private parlors. Rates of board from $3.00 to $4.00 per day, $15 to $25 per week, according to location of room and season. Private parlors and baths extra. Special rates by the month, or early in the season. Information regarding terms, etc., will be promptly furnished upon application.

A fine Orchestra engaged for the season.

O. M. SHAW & SON,

Proprietors West End Hotel,

OPEN FROM JULY 1, TO SEPT. 15.   **BAR HARBOR, ME.**

MARLBOROUGH HOTEL,

BAR HARBOR, MAINE.

S. N. HIGGINS, : : Manager.

CENTRALLY LOCATED.

SURROUNDED BY BEAUTIFUL LAWNS.

HANDSOMELY FURNISHED.

Large Music Room and Parlors.

HAS ELECTRIC BELLS & ELECTRIC LIGHTS.

Open During the Summer Months.

The ✱ Grand ✱ Central.

✱ ✱ ✱

➤CENTRALLY ✱ LOCATED.⬅

Surrounded by a large well-kept Lawn.

The house will accommodate 350 guests and is supplied with all the conveniences of a first-class hotel.

ELECTRIC LIGHTS,   ELECTRIC BELLS,
EXCELLENT CUISINE   AND   EFFICIENT SERVICE.

For terms etc., apply to

R. HAMOR & SONS, Proprietors.

The Newport,

W. M. ROBERTS, : PROPRIETOR.
BAR HARBOR, MAINE.

Open About June 1st.

* * *

THE NEWPORT IS BEAUTIFULLY LOCATED NEAR THE CLUB HOUSE,

AND FROM ITS VERANDAHS A MAGNIFICENT VIEW OF THE HARBOR CAN BE HAD.

MOST PROMINENT AMONG MT. DESERT'S MANY ATTRACTIONS
—IS—
GREEN MOUNTAIN AND ITS RAILWAY.

The trip from Bar Harbor to the Summit takes about an hour and a half, and includes a

SHORT STAGE RIDE TO EAGLE LAKE,
A SAIL BY STEAMBOAT ACROSS THE LAKE,
THENCE BY RAILWAY TO SUMMIT.

Six Round Trips Every Day.

Lunch served at all hours at the Hotel on the Summit. Special trips for excursion parties.

FARE, ROUND TRIP ONE DOLLAR.

GREEN MOUNTAIN RAILWAY,
M. H. WARDWELL, Gen'l Manager.

TICKET OFFICE, MAIN ST., BAR HARBOR.   GENERAL OFFICE, BANGOR, MAINE.

WALL COTTAGE DINING HALL.
COTTAGE STREET.

This Dining Hall is run in connection with the well-known Wall's Cottage, and we are prepared to furnish

Board by the Day or Week.

Also meals at all hours. Every pains taken for the comfort of guests. Pleasant rooms can be obtained in the Cottage on reasonable terms. For further particulars inquire of

MRS. C. E. SOUTHARD, Wall Cottage.

J. M. Brown's Bakery,
COR. MAIN AND WEST STS.,

Bar Harbor,   -   -   -   Maine.

BREAD & PASTRY of all KINDS, WEDDING CAKE MADE TO ORDER.
Excursion Parties Supplied with Lunches.
Also a fine assortment of CONFECTIONERY Fresh every day.
☞ ALL GOODS DELIVERED.

METEOROLOGICAL SUMMARY,
FOR THE MONTH OF AUGUST, 1889. GREEN MOUNTAIN STATION.

Date.	Mean.	Maximum.	Minimum.	Precipitation in Inches and Hundredths.
1	66	69	62	.12
2	62	72	53	.04
3	64	68	59	T.
4	66	72	59	0
5	60	66	53	.03
6	59	66	52	0
7	60	65	55	.04
8	56	63	49	.16
9	58	61	56	.01
10	62	68	57	.09
11	59	64	54	0
12	52	58	46	0
13	54	63	46	T.
14	52	54	50	.36
15	54	58	51	.35
16	57	60	54	.02
17	60	65	54	0
18	60	66	54	0
19	62	67	58	0
20	64	70	57	0
21	62	67	58	0
22	64	71	56	.08
23	62	68	57	0
24	60	65	56	0
25	58	61	55	0
26	54	59	50	0
27	56	60	52	0
28	59	66	52	0
29	64	68	60	0
30	64	71	56	0
31	66	72	59	0

SUMMARY.

Mean barometer, 30.053; highest barometer, 30.399, date, 27th; lowest barometer, 29.786, date, 15th; mean temperature, 59.9; highest temperature, 72, date, 31st; lowest temperature, 46, date, 12th; greatest daily range of temperature, 19 on 2nd; least daily range of temperature, 4 on 14th. Prevailing direction of wind, S. W., 42°; total movement of wind, 12317. Extreme velocity of wind, direction and date, 60, S. W. on 3d. Total precipitation, 1.30 inches; number of days on which .01 inch or more of precipitation fell, 11. Number of cloudless days, 9; partly cloudy, 10; cloudy days, 12.

E. P. JONES, Corp'l Signal Corps.

Note. Barometer reduced to sea level. "T" indicates trace of rainfall.

M. GALLERT & CO.,

—DEALER IN—

FOREIGN AND DOMESTIC

Dry, Fancy & Furnishing Goods,

Hamor Block,

BAR HARBOR, : : MAINE.

Sproul's Market;

MAIN ST., BAR HARBOR, MAINE.

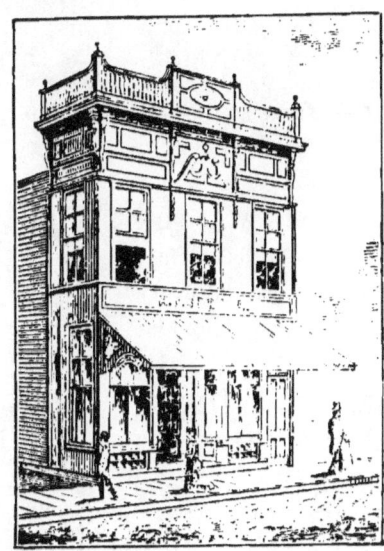

This well-known market has been

Established Twenty Years,

and during that time it has supplied

MEATS,
VEGETABLES,
—AND—

GENERAL MARKET SUPPLIES,

to the principal families who have spent summers here. We have in connection with the market a Large Farm and Hot Houses, from which the Market is supplied DAILY with

FRESH VEGETABLES, ETC.,

Such vegetables are much to be preferred to those shipped here from the cities, as they are not old and withered.

ALSO POULTRY and EGGS,
Fresh from the Farm.

DEERFOOT FARM BUTTER,

Received in small quantities to insure freshness.

YOUR PATRONAGE IS RESPECTFULLY SOLICITED.

Morton's CHOCOLATES AND BON BONS, are the best in the world, and fresh every day at the "Rose and Lily."

Morton's CREAM MINTS, MAPLE CREAMS, and other flavors are the ONLY CREAM MINTS in Bar Harbor that are soft and creamy, being free from grains or crystals of sugar, and made fresh every day.

CHOICE ROSES AND ALL THE BEST FLOWERS for fine decorating, for Dinner Parties, for all and every occasion, can always be found at "The Rose and Lily."

W. E. MORTON & CO., "SOCIETY FLORISTS," OPPOSITE RODICK, MAIN ST.

"The Rose and Lily."

OVINGTON BROTHERS.

FINE TABLE CHINA, CUT GLASS, STERLING SILVER,
WROUGHT IRON,
DINNER, TEA AND TOILET SETS,
FIRE SETS, AND ANDIRONS,
PARLOR & BANQUET LAMPS,
CANDLESTICKS.

OVINGTON BROTHERS,

MAIN STREET, · · **BAR HARBOR,**

——ALSO AT——

330 Fifth Avenue, New York,   250 Fulton Street, Brooklyn.
33 Rue de Parodis, Paris.

ESTABLISHED 1840.
ISAAC LOCKE & CO.,
PRODUCE COMMISSION MERCHANTS,
WHOLESALE AND RETAIL DEALERS IN
FOREIGN & DOMESTIC FRUITS,
VEGETABLES AND HOT HOUSE PRODUCTIONS.
PICKLES AND PICKLED LIMES. FINE OLIVE OIL.

97, 99 & 101 Faneuil Hall Market, Boston,
——AND——
DUNBAR BLOCK, : Bar Harbor, Me.
Mr. A. T. Cumings

Will, as heretofore, manage our business at Bar Harbor, and as we give special attention to

HOTEL, CLUB, AND FINE FAMILY TRADE,

We shall be pleased to give our patrons in Bar Harbor the benefit to be derived from so direct connection with the Boston market.

L. H. TREVETT,   A. W. MARSHALL.

TREVETT & MARSHALL,
TRUCKMEN,

Would respectfully announce to the people that they are again on deck and are prepared to do all kinds of trucking, such as transporting baggage, trunks, furniture, freight, etc., promptly and properly.

MOVING PIANOS

Will receive their especial attention. Teams always on the wharf at the arrival of every boat. YOUR PATRONAGE IS SOLICITED.

TREVETT & MARSHALL.

Height of Our Mountains.

	Feet.		Feet.
Green Mountain,	1527	Robinson's	700
Sargent's "	1344	Dog	670
Dry "	1268	The Beehive,	540
Pemetic "	1262	Great Pond Hill,	540
Newport "	1060	The Cleft { North,	610
Western " { W. Peak,	1073	{ South,	460
{ E. Peak,	971	Peak of Otter,	506
The White Cap,	925	Carter's Nubble,	480
Brown's Mountain,	860	Interlaken Hill,	462
The Bubbles { North,	815	Mt. Kebo,	405
{ South,	780	Jordan's Hill, { North,	340
Beech Mountain,	855	{ South,	360
McFarland's Mountain,	761	Flying Mountain,	300
Great Hill,	748	Bald Mountain,	250
The Triad { East,	720	High Head Mountain,	208
{ North,	688	Burnt Mountain,	175
{ South,	600	Mt. Gibbon,	160
Young's Mountain,	706	Otter Cliff,	112

CONNERS BROS.,

Have at their wharf at the Foot of Main St.,

BOATS OF EVERY DESCRIPTION,

Which will be LET BY THE WEEK, DAY, HOUR OR SEASON.

Cat-rigs, Sloops, Canoes and Row-boats,
And the STEAMER CREEDMOOR.

Experienced Guides and Boatmen furnished if desired.

The Louisburg,

BAR HARBOR, MAINE.

M. L. BALCH, Proprietor,
　　J. ALBERT BUTLER, Manager.

OPEN FROM JUNE 30th TO SEPT. 15th.

Renowned for its superior Table and Attentive Service. A celebrated Chef and Steward in charge of their respective departments. Morning and evening Concerts by an Orchestra of solo artists popular in society circles.

SPECIALTIES:	RATES:
COLORED SERVICE, PRIVATE CATERING, WAITERS FOR DINNERS, RECEPTIONS & COLLATIONS, TABLE D' HOTE DINNER, 6:30 TO 8 P. M.	JULY, $4, $4.50 and $5 per day. AUGUST, $5.00 per day. SEPT., $4, $4.50 and $5 per day. Special rates for families for July and for the Season.

W. A. MILLIKEN,

WHOLESALE AND RETAIL DEALER IN

COAL, WOOD AND CHARCOAL,

ALL KINDS OF WOOD SAWED BY MACHINE AND SPLIT, READY FOR USE.

Steam Dry House, for Drying and Preparing Wood.
　　Fairbank's Platform Scales, for weighing Hay, Horses, etc.

GRAVEL FOR STREETS, DRIVEWAYS, ETC., FOR SALE.

Office and Wharf, West Street, near West End Hotel,

Bar Harbor, 　　:　　:　　Maine.

The Malvern Hotel,

—AND—

COTTAGES.

* * *

GEO. H. CARTER, : MANAGER.

BILLIARD HALL

—AND—

Hair-Dressing Rooms.

Main St., Opposite the Marlborough Hotel,

UP ONE FLIGHT.

* * *

ESTABLISHED 1883.

GRANT, BARBOUR & LADD,

FINE BOOTS AND SHOES,

Men's Soft and Stiff Hats,

RUBBER GOODS, UMBRELLAS, ETC.

We make a specialty of

LIGHT COLORED LOW AND HIGH SHOES.

Men's & Boys' Solid Rubber Sole Tennis, Oxfords & Bals.

A good assortment of

LADIES', MISSES' & CHILDREN'S TENNIS SHOES.

Mount Desert Block,

BAR HARBOR, - - **MAINE.**

1868. 1890.

TOBIAS L. ROBERTS,

EAST SIDE MAIN STREET.

NEW CANNED GOODS,

PURE LEAF LARD.

FRESH EGGS, THE CHOICEST BUTTER.

Apollinaris and Lithia Water.

CROCKERY, TIN AND WOODEN WARE.

Everything in Fine Groceries.

* * *

HAY AND RYE STRAW. **BEST QUALITY WHITE OATS.**

F. D. FOSTER,

HOUSE, SIGN AND DECORATIVE PAINTER.

PAPER HANGING.

PAINTING WALLS AND CEILINGS In Water Colors a Specialty.

DEALER IN PAINTS & VARNISHES, PLATE & WINDOW GLASS.

Office, 136 Main Sreet.   Shop Cor. Main and First South Street·

Mr. Foster has done work for me for many years. I have always found him prompt, painstaking and reasonable in his charges.

W. R. EMERSON, Architect.

CHAS. C. BURRILL,

GENERAL INSURANCE AGENT,

HEAD OFFICE. 16 State St., Ellsworth, Me.

CORRESPONDENCE SOLICITED.

ASSETS REPRESENTED AT THIS AGENCY OVER $66,000,000.

Partial List of Companies Represented,

ÆTNA INSURANCE CO., of Hartford, Conn.
PHŒNIX INSURANCE CO., of Hartford, Conn.
HOME INSURANCE CO., of New York, N. Y.
HANOVER FIRE INSURANCE CO., of New York, N. Y.
GERMAN AMERICAN INSURANCE CO., of New York, N. Y.
INSURANCE CO. OF NORTH AMERICA, of Philadelphia, Pa.
SPRINGFIELD FIRE AND MARINE INSURANCE CO., of Springfield, Mass.
LIVERPOOL, LONDON AND GLOBE INSURANCE CO., of London, Eng.
IMPERIAL FIRE INSURANCE CO., of London, Eng.
NEW HAMPSHIRE FIRE INSURANCE CO., of Manchester, N. H.
GRANITE STATE FIRE INSURANCE CO., of Portsmouth, N. H.
UNION MUTUAL LIFE INSURANCE CO., of Portland, Me.
TRAVELERS' LIFE AND ACCIDENT INSURANCE CO., of Hartford, Conn.

Branch Office, **BUNKER BLOCK**, Opposite Rodick House.

Bar Harbor, - Maine.

S. D. WIGGIN,

PRESCRIPTION ✳ DRUGGIST.

Opposite Rodick's,

J. H. DUNCAN,
—DEALER IN—
Groceries & Provisions.

I AM ALSO AGENT FOR THE
HAMPDEN SWEET CREAM
FRESH EVERY DAY at my store on LEDGE LAWN AVENUE.

Mount Desert.

Tall granite peaks ascend towards Heaven's blue dome,
And Neptune's waters lash the rocky shores,
Where thou, fair island, rises from the wave;
And lovely lakes, set in fair groves of green,
Adorn thy breast like jewels of great price,
And charm the eyes of woodland wanderers.
Dark woods, and lovely meadows, where the sun
Lights up the landscape with a lovely hue,
Divide between them the delight of mind;
And pleasant roads, bedight with fairest flowers,
Recall to mind the paths of Paradise.
Here pensive melancholy, and light-hearted joy,
Find sweet employ midst Nature's handiwork.
O, lovely isle of hill and dale,
Of sea-beat shore, and marge of peaceful lake,
Here Nature has been lavish with her charms,
And decked thee with outstretched arms.
Well may we say with one of earlier age
"Infinite riches" grace thy "little room."

WILLIAM M. SILBER.

NICKERSON & SPRATT,
—DEALERS IN—
HAY, STRAW AND GRAIN.
ALL KINDS OF MILL FEED ALWAYS ON HAND.

We have rented the storehouse on Bunker's wharf and as we buy hay and straw direct of the farmer, and have it transferred by vessel, can handle it at bottom prices.

MILL AND STORE ON SOUTH STREET.
TELEPHONE CONNECTION.

ROBINSON,

OUTFITTING ✻ NOVELTIES,

And all kinds of

GENTLEMEN'S FURNISHING GOODS.

✻ ✻ ✻

SILK, FLANNEL, CHEVOIT AND MADRAS NEGLIGEE SHIRTS IN ENDLESS VARIETY.

FLANNEL TENNIS COATS, AND SUITS, SILK SASHES AND BELTS, LADIES' BLAZERS & BLOUSES, CHILDREN'S JERSEY AND SAILOR SUITS.

A Complete Assortment of

MEN'S NECKWEAR, GLOVES, HOSIERY,

UNDERWEAR, DRESS SHIRTS, NIGHT SHIRTS,

PAJAMAS, UMBRELLAS, CANES, ETC.

Soft and Stiff Hats, Coachmen's Hats, Straw Hats, Ladies' Sailor Hats, Etc.

✻ ✻ ✻

◁CUSTOM TAILORING DEPARTMENT.▷

Clothing Cleansed, Pressed & Repaired.

Special attention paid to cleansing Flannels.

✻ ✻ ✻

JAMES A. ROBINSON,

PORCUPINE BUILDING, BAR HARBOR,

WHEELWRIGHT & CLARK'S BLOCK, BANGOR, ME.

Bar Harbor Banking & Trust Co

Mount Desert Block, Bar Harbor, Me.

* * *

Cash Capital, $50,000.00.   Surplus, $6,000.00.

Liability of Stockholders, $50,000.00.

* * *

OFFICERS:	TRUSTEES
A. P. WISWELL, President.	A. P. Wiswell, E. H. Greely,
L. B. DEASY, Vice President.	Fred C. Lynam, L. B. Deasy,
FRED C. LYNAM, Treasurer.	Jno. Biddle Porter. C. S. Leflingwell,
E. J. TORREY, Assistant Treasurer.	W. P. Foster.
JNO. T. HIGGINS, Secretary.	

CHECKS AND DRAFTS CASHED.

DEPOSITS SOLICITED SUBJECT TO CHECK.

◁WILLIAM FENNELLY,▷

Hamor's Block, - Bar Harbor, Me.

MANUFACTURER AND DEALER IN

HARNESSES,

Blankets, Robes, Whips

——AND——

→HORSE * FURNISHING * GOODS←

Comprising everything needed for the Horse or Stable.

Long experience has taught me the wants of my customers, and summer visitors will find at my store everything usually kept in a first-class Harness Store, at prices lower than the usual city prices.

CHAS. C. BURRILL, President.   EDGAR F. BREWER, Cashier.
WILLIAM ROGERS, Vice President.

THE FIRST NATIONAL BANK.

Rodick Block, Bar Harbor, Me.

Fully Equipped for Every Kind of Legitimate Banking.

CAPITAL, $50,000.00.

We respectfully solicit accounts of Bankers, Merchants, Lumbermen, Business Men and others, and will cheerfully extend every favor consistent with sound Banking.

DIRECTORS—WILLIAM ROGERS, M.D., EUGENE B. RICHARDS, BLITHEN S. HIGGINS, CHAS. C. BURRILL, JOHN ANDREW RODICK, NATHAN CLEAVES.

CORRESPONDENCE SOLICITED.

MUSIC STORE,
S. J. CLEMENT,   -   AGENT.

* * *

Pianos, Organs and all kinds of Musical Instruments and General Musical Merchandise,

—ALSO—

SEWING MACHINES, to sell and to rent, AND SEWING MACHINE SUPPLIES.

—* FIRST-CLASS PIANOS TO LET. *—

RODICK BLOCK, CORNER MAIN AND COTTAGE STREETS,

BAR HARBOR, ME.

MORAN BROTHERS,
◁ MERCHANT ✳ TAILORS, ▷
—AND DEALERS IN—
GENT'S FURNISHINGS.   TENNIS GOODS
A SPECIALTY.

BUNKER BLOCK,   -   BAR HARBOR, ME.

SUNSET LEDGE,
Most Beautiful unoccupied hill-side site in Bar Harbor,
FOR SALE.

The lot contains two and one-half acres of land on the northerly side of Malden Hill, near the residence of Mrs. R. B. Scott. From it there is an unobstructed view of the village, Frenchman's Bay with its islands, and the mountains on Mount Desert and the mainland. A broad private way for a carriage road leads to Kebo street, and a foot path communicates with Eagle Lake road, over which an eight or ten minutes' walk will bring one to Mount Desert street or the Malvern Hotel. The lot is covered with a fine healthy growth of large trees, and at a small cost the grounds can be changed into wooded lawns, driveways and a tennis court. The new Acadia Park and the Kebo Valley Club House are near at hand and to them runs a road to Malden Hill. As all the estates in the immediate vicinity of Sunset Ledge are owned by non-residents there is no danger of objectionable buildings being erected near it. For prices and terms apply to

Dr. Wm. Rogers, Bar Harbor, Me.

ALFRED G. CURTIS,
DRUGGIST.

MAIN STREET,   -   BAR HARBOR.

Registered.

W. B. HIGGINS,

✳ DEALER IN ✳

Meats of All Kinds,

FRESH POULTRY & GAME,

BUTTER, CHEESE, EGGS AND CREAM.

✳ ✳ ✳

Having leased one-half of the handsome store in DUNBAR BLOCK, I am prepared to furnish customers with

CHOICE ✳ MARKET ✳ SUPPLIES

At Reasonable Prices.

✳ ✳ ✳

ORDERS ✳ BY ✳ TELEPHONE ✳ PROMPTLY ✳ FILLED.

W. B. HIGGINS,
DUNBAR BLOCK, MAIN STREET.

HER LETTER.

Written During the Height of the Season at Bar Harbor.

You asked me to write you a letter
  Detailing the gaieties here;
I have tried to write sooner, but couldn't.
  I hope you will pardon me dear.
But now that I've put pen to paper,
  I mean to report all the news;
How we boat, flirt and ride, through the season,
  And the various ways to amuse.

All the world and his wife are here present,
  And the season's as gay as can be;
While the gayest in all the bright *cortege*
  Is your humble subscriber, poor me.
For I've danced and I've flirted and *feted*
  And turned the night into day;
And the wonder of all to me, dearest,
  Is why I've not fainted away,

At the sight of such splendor and fashion—
  For you know, dear, it's not so at home.
How I wish that the summer was longer,
  How jolly, forever, to roam
In this island of lake and of mountain,
  Where life is one long pleasant dream,
And the shadows of life are forgotten
  Save to render the contrast supreme.

We are now in the height of the season;
  This week will be best of them all,
For each day there is something or other,
  A *fete*, a reception or ball.
There are hops every night at the houses,
  And the Germans are strictly *au fait*,
While the dinners and luncheons are splendid
  And the picnics are ever so gay.

I have danced at the Rodick and Malvern,
  Have lunched at Sorrento *Cafe*,
Been received by the Whitneys and Shepards,
  And rode in a wagon of hay;
I have been to Canoe Club receptions,
  And acted in private charades,
Taken part in a play at the Rodick,
  And gone off on canoe escapades.

My yachting experience is varied,
  I have tried every one that is here
From the Sagamore steam yacht so stately,
  To the Kathleen, the sweet little dear.

I *do* like these yachtsmen, they're splendid,
  With their caps and their buttons so fine:
I think that if ever I marry,
  A yachtsman will be in my line.

And oh, I had almost forgotten,
  Our beautiful strolls by the shore,
When the moonlight gleams over the waters,
  And the noise of the old ocean's roar
Is hushed as it kisses the pebbles,
  As the touch of a sweetheart's kiss
Will still the dark tempest of passion
  And waft the receiver to bliss.

There now, I have told you my secret,
  I said *our* in that last verse, I know;
But please, do not tell it to Harry,
  For he never was really my beau;
I have known him so long, he seems rather
  A brother or cousin at most,
And I don't think he cares for me either
  For he flirts with that Evelyn Post.

Now dear, don't you tell him, and surely,
  If you visit Bar Harbor next week,
I will make you acquainted at once, dear,
  With the notable men of our clique.
You shall dine with the Baron on Sunday,
  Have the *entree* to Mossley Hall,
Hobnob with the Whitneys and Shepards,
  And dance with the Count at the ball.

You may flirt with the dudes at the Rodick,
  Play lawn tennis, canoe and all that;
Take your chicken and champagne at Sproul's,
  Go to church and exhibit your hat.
Perhaps you may find a rich lover,
  For I know you deserve such a fate;
And the thanks will be due to the writer,
  Your ever affectionate   KATE.

P. S. I'm engaged to be married
  To the youth whom I met on the rocks;
But until I shall give you permission,
  Don't mention a word to our folks.
He has plenty of money, a steam yacht,
  A rent roll exceedingly high,
And he says he will come to Bar Harbor
  Every year for the summer. Good-bye!

ALICK J. GRANT,
In Bar Harbor Record.

BLITHEN S. HIGGINS,

GROCER.

LARGEST AND FINEST STOCK IN TOWN.

—— ALSO DEALER IN ——

Hay, Straw, Oats, Middlings, Etc.

MAIN STREET.

BAR HARBOR, : : MAINE.

CLEAVES BROS.'
LIVERY AND BOARDING STABLE,

COTTAGE STREET, BAR HARBOR, ME.

SEVENTY-FIVE HORSES.   CARRIAGES ALL NEW.

BUCKBOARDS, CABRIOLETS, DOG-CARTS,

Buck-road Wagons, Ladies' Phaetons, Buggies, Etc.

SINGLE, DOUBLE AND FOUR-IN-HAND HITCHES.

EXPERIENCED COACHMEN (IN LIVERY) FURNISHED WHEN WANTED

HORSES BOARDED BY THE DAY, WEEK OR SEASON.

TELEPHONE CONNECTION.

A TALE OF MOUNT DESERT.

BAR HARBOR DAYS. A Tale of Mount Desert. By Mrs. Burton Harrison. Illustrated. pp. 190. 16mo, Ornamental Cloth, $1.25.

A bright and pretty summer story, crisply written, and interesting and attractive in the reading. . Wholly readable and entertaining.—[Saturday Evening Gazette, Boston.
A bright story of life at Mount Desert. . . . It is exceedingly well done, and the scenery, the ways of the people, and the social methods of the rusticators lend interest to the book.—[Christian Advocate, N. Y.
The book is bright and readable. —[Courier, Boston.
The narrative is bright and sparkling---[Boston Journal.

A delightful book about Mount Desert, its summer inhabitants, their sayings and doings.—[N. Y. Sun.
One of the most attractive books of the season, and will be in great demand by readers who wish an original, captivating summer idyl.-[Hartford Post.
A very charming story.—[New Orleans States.
A charming little book, which causes the erroneous desert to blossom as the rose.—[N. Y. Star.

Published by HARPER & BROTHERS, New York.

The above work will be sent by mail, postage prepaid, to any part of the United States, Canada, or Mexico, on receipt of the price.

HIGGINS & MARCYES,
Successors to Chas. A. Ingalls,

LANDSCAPE GARDENERS ᴬᴺᴰ CONTRACTORS,

Construction of Tennis Grounds and Avenues, and Draining a Specialty.

Tennis Grounds Marked and Rolled With a Horse-roller.

——LAWNS CARED FOR BY THE SEASON.——

All kinds of Shrubbery, Vines and Evergreens furnished when sufficient notice is given.

Huyler's
FINE ✲ CONFECTIONS.
BON-BONS, CHOCOLATES,
FROM 863 BROADWAY, NEW YORK.

On Sale at 5 PORCUPINE BLOCK, BAR HARBOR, from June 1st to Nov. 1st.

To have our table well supplied with all the delicacies of the season, as well as with the necessaries, is one of the chief enjoyments of living, and we would say to our summer patrons that it is our aim to be able to supply their every want in this direction, from the best sources and at reasonable prices. Everything in the line of

Groceries AND Dairy Products

can be found at our store. We also keep on hand a good supply of provender of all kinds and of the best grades, for horses. Your patronage is respectfully solicited.

✻ **R. H. KITTREDGE & CO.,** ✻
Mount Desert Street,   :   BAR HARBOR, MAINE.

STAFFORD'S LIVERY STABLE,

SPRING ST., BAR HARBOR.

The Proprietor has been making extensive arrangements for the coming season, and is prepared to supply his former patrons and the public in general with

Carriages of Every Description,

With Elegant Horses and Competent and Intelligent Drivers in Livery.

BY THE HOUR, DAY OR SEASON.

The Nickerson Stable, corner Mt. Desert and Eden streets, will be kept by Mr. Stafford, solely as a Boarding Stable for Visitors' Horses.

ANDREW STAFFORD.

TELEPHONE CONNECTION.

J. E. TRIPP,

DOUBLE AND SINGLE
Buckboards, ✸ Carriages, ✸ Cutunders, ✸ Etc.

Furnished at short notice, with or without driver, night or day. None but experienced drivers employed.

TEAMS TO LET FOR THE SEASON.
HORSES BOARDED BY THE WEEK OR SEASON.

STABLE ON LEDGE LAWN AVE.,   BAR HARBOR. ME.

TELEPHONE CONNECTION.

STETSON FOSTER,
Upholsterer & Cabinet Maker.
◁WINDOW SHADES,▷
FURNITURE, AWNINGS, STRAW MATTINGS

And Importer of the Fayal Willow furniture and Stuffs for Summer Curtains & furnishings.

13 SUMMER ST., BOSTON.   **BAR HARBOR, ME.**

HANCOCK COUNTY TELEPHONE CO.
Central Office at Bar Harbor.

With Branch Offices at Ellsworth and the other principal towns in Hancock County.

AND EXCHANGES WITH BANGOR, ROCKLAND AND BELFAST.

Prompt and Efficient Service.

The Bar Harbor Exchange has about 140 subscribers, and has telephone connection with the Hotels, Banks, Express Offices, and Railroad and Steamship Offices.

CENTRAL OFFICE, ROOM 20,
MOUNT DESERT BLOCK,   :   **MAIN STREET.**

FOSTER'S,
FINE ✷ STATIONERY,
FANCY GOODS,
PAPER ✷ HANGINGS, ✷ TOYS, ✷ ETC.

136 MAIN STREET,
—OPPOSITE THE RODICK.—

F. E. SHERMAN,
MAIN STREET, - **BAR HARBOR, ME.**

CHOICE FRUIT AND CONFECTIONERY.

ALL THE LEADING BRANDS OF FINE CUT AND PLUG TOBACCOS, CIGARS & CIGARETTES.

"TWENTY-FIVE ASSOCIATES" CIGAR is the best in town for 5 Cts.

FINE STATIONERY.

A. G. BULGER,
—DEALER IN—

FINE GROCERIES, FLOUR AND GRAIN,
Selected Tea, Pure Coffee and Spices,

BUTTER AND CHEESE FROM the BEST VERMONT and MAINE DAIRIES

FOREIGN AND DOMESTIC FRUITS, CANNED GOODS.

Furniture, Carpetings, Straw Mattings and Oil Cloths, Crockery and Glass Ware, Oil Stoves, Etc.

COTTAGE STREET, - **BAR HARBOR, ME.**

ERNEST EMERY,
PHOTOGRAPHER.
FINE LINE OF VIEWS.

*PHOTOGRAPHS MADE & ENLARGED. ARTISTS' MATERIAL.
EXTERIOR & INTERIOR VIEWS MADE TO ORDER.*

MAIN STREET, : BAR HARBOR.

C. C. SOPER & SON'S
SUCCESSORS TO SOPER & HIGGINS.

✳ MARKET. ✳

COTTAGE STREET, BAR HARBOR, MAINE.

CHOICE ✳ MEATS ✳ OF ✳ ALL ✳ KINDS.

Poultry & Game, Butter & Eggs.

VEGETABLES, FRUIT AND CANNED GOODS.

We sell only the best, and respectfully solicit the patronage of those who want fine goods at reasonable prices.

C. C. SOPER & SON.

GOODWIN'S,
Bar Harbor, : : Maine.

Opp. The Marlborough, near Cor. Cottage & Main Sts.

THE BEST HAIR DRESSING ROOMS IN MAINE.

FOUR CHAIRS RUN BY FIRST-CLASS PROFESSIONAL HAIR DRESSERS.

CHOICE BRANDS OF CIGARS AND TOBACCOS.

Mr. Goodwin is also proprietor of the Hair Dressing Rooms at the RODICK AND WEST END. Ladies' and Children's Hair Cutting and Shampooing a specialty. Calls from Cottages and Hotels will receive prompt attention. Mr. Goodwin will be found during the summer months at the Rodick.

FRED C. LYNAM & CO.,
FIRE INSURANCE AGENTS.
Office with BAR HARBOR BANKING & TRUST CO.

BAR HARBOR, : : : **MAINE.**

The best English & American Co's represented.
THE ONLY ESTABLISHED AGENCY IN BAR HARBOR.

→B. BRADLEY,←
Successor of Suminsby & Bradley.

—DEALER IN—

Ladies' & Gent's Fine Boots & Shoes.

Gent's Furnishing Goods,

HATS AND CAPS,

NECKWEAR, MEN'S AND BOYS' CLOTHING,

UMBRELLAS, ETC. ETC.

COR. COTTAGE AND MAIN STREETS, BAR HARBOR.

C. S. GREEN,   B. C. REYNOLDS.

GREEN & REYNOLDS,
MANUFACTURERS OF AND DEALERS IN

Furnaces, Stoves, Ranges and Tinware,

ALSO DEALERS IN KITCHEN FURNISHING GOODS,
WOODEN WARE, etc. Agents for EDDY'S REFRIGERATORS.

JOB WORK PROMPTLY ATTENDED TO.

Main Street,   :   **Bar Harbor, Maine.**

James G. Blaine's Arrival.

"The Rambler" of the RECORD describes Mr. Blaine's trip last spring from the terminus of the Maine Central Railroad to Bar Harbor, in the following very beautiful style:

"There are thousands of places like these in the world, but only one Bar Harbor!" So said the Man from Maine the other evening as he stood in the pilot house of the magnificent steamer Sappho and gazed out upon the beauties of Frenchman's Bay. His attention had been called by Captain Oliver to Sullivan Harbor and Sorrento as the boat was fast leaving them behind. With a swift, casual glance at those budding summer resorts, Mr. Blaine uttered the remark I have just quoted, and then, with the field glasses which he held in his hand, he swept the coast of Mount Desert, striving to get a glimpse of the towers of his beautiful summer residence, Stanwood. I have never seen Mr. Blaine looking better. He seemed as happy as some big school boy just let loose on his summer vacation. A little pale, perhaps, owing to the severe heat and trying weather which he had just left behind him in Washington; but the dark eyes were flashing and the voice had a clear ring in it that betokened a wondrous vitality and a pleasurable excitement in the anticipation of his long holiday. It was truly a remarkable scene. The sun was nearing the western horizon and the mountains were beginning to cast their dark shadows over the peaceful waters of the Bay. The wooded slopes on the eastern shore of Mount Desert were already in the shade, but old Sol's rays still lighted up the opposite coast and sparkled in the windows of the buildings at Sorrento. From out the dark mass of foliage which crowned the foot hills above Eden street, peeped forth the turrets and chimneys of many a handsome cottage; while the residences along the shores stood out in bold relief from their emerald setting of lawns and shrubberies. Beyond, towered the hoary head of Green Mountain, with the Queen of Summer Resorts, looking, in the distance, like an enchanted city of palaces, nestling in the wooded plateau at its base. Methinks the ancient mariners who first explored this state, were gifted, unconsciously, with the spirit of prophecy, and the fabulous city of Norombega was but a prefiguration of this Eden of the West. Across the mouth of the Bay lay the rocky chain of the Porcupines, relieved here and there by a blue strip of ocean stretching away into the distance till sea and sky seemed to blend in azure. To the northward a narrow arm of the Bay wound like a thread of silver between the low shores of Lamoine and the grassy slopes of Mount Desert, till it lost itself in the Narrows; and far beyond, its summit kissed by the lingering rays of the sun, rose the lofty dome of Blue Hill. Tiny, white-winged crafts glided over the dancing waters of the Bay; and in the centre of this beautiful picture was the Sappho, bearing toward his island home Maine's favorite son and America's foremost statesman. Uttered on the impulse of the moment, with the fairest scene on all God's footstool before him, his words carried conviction with them; and there is one, at least, of his audience who henceforth will say with Blaine, ' "There is but one Bar Harbor." '

Bar Harbor Record.

A BRIGHT, ENTERPRISING AND ORIGINAL WEEKLY NEWSPAPER,

Devoted to the Best Interests of Mount Desert Island and Hancock County.

* * *

During the Summer Months the RECORD contains an ably edited

✷ SOCIETY ✷ DEPARTMENT, ✷

giving the doings of the summer visitors to Mount Desert Island and the Frenchman's Bay resorts.

The RECORD is pronounced by many to be the best weekly newspaper published outside of the cities.

SUBSCRIPTION RATES : PUBLISHED THURSDAYS.
$1.50 a year. Office, Mount Desert Block,
$1.00 for six months. BAR HARBOR, ME.

W. H. SHERMAN, Managing Editor.

Bar Harbor Steam Laundry,

(Opposite West End Hotel.)

J. F. Hodgkins,
Proprietor.

COTTAGE AND YACHT WORK A SPECIALTY.

TELEPHONE CONNECTION.

J. F. HODGKINS,

—DEALER IN—

Fish of all Kinds,

WEST STREET,

Bar Harbor, Me.

TELEPHONE CONNECTION.

FRANK P. MOORE,
—DEALER IN—
WATCHES, CLOCKS AND JEWELRY,
Spectacles & Eye-glasses. Silver & Plated Ware.

French Clocks Repaired.   Fine Watch Repairing a Specialty.

BRADLEY BLOCK, MAIN STREET,

Bar Harbor, : : : Maine.

J. E. CLARK,
BOARDING, HACK & LIVERY STABLE.

* * *

Buckboards, Cutunders, Dog-carts, Buck-Road Wagons, Ladies' Phaetons and Buggies.

Single, Double and Four-in-hand Hitches.

* * *

Teams Let by Day, Month or Season.

* * *

HIGH STREET, NEAR MOUNT DESERT STREET.

TELEPHONE CONNECTION.

OSMOND EMERY,
HOUSE, FURNITURE AND SIGN PAINTER.
—DEALER IN—
PAINTS, OILS AND PAPER HANGINGS.
COTTAGE ST., NEAR HOLLAND AVE., BAR HARBOR.

Painters, Paper Hangers and Kalsominers furnished at short notice.

J. E. Clark,

CONTRACTOR AND BUILDER.

All Orders Promptly Attended To.

—— ALSO ——

PLANS FURNISHED & ESTIMATES GIVEN.

OFFICE AND SHOP, HIGH STREET.

TELEPHONE CONNECTION.

At Hull's Cove, Maine, you can find

BREWER & HAMOR,

Who carry a Large Stock of

FANCY GROCERIES, DRY GOODS,

BOOTS AND SHOES,

WOOD, COAL and GENERAL MERCHANDISE.

DE GRASSE FOX,

REAL ESTATE AGENT.

BAR HARBOR OFFICE,
  MT. DESERT & KEBO STS.

PHILADELPHIA OFFICE,
  201 SOUTH 11TH STREET.

DEASY & HIGGINS,

Attorneys at Law,

ROOMS 2, 3 AND 4

MOUNT DESERT BLOCK,

BAR HARBOR, ME.

Notary Public.
  Commissioner of Deeds.

W. P. FOSTER,
ATTORNEY
—AND—
COUNSELOR AT LAW.
ROOMS 3 & 4, HAMOR BLOCK.
NOTARY PUBLIC.
BAR HARBOR, : ME.

E. S. CLARK,
ATTORNEY AT LAW,
—OFFICES IN—
Rodick Block, Bar Harbor.

Special attention given to collections

Justice of the Peace. Notary Public.

E. B. RICHARDS,
REAL ESTATE AGENT.
FURNISHED COTTAGES
TO RENT.
Bunker Block, Bar Harbor.

MR. A. D. ADDISON,
OF WASHINGTON.
Has succeeded Mr. Augustine Heard in the
REAL ESTATE BUSINESS
AT BAR HARBOR.

Mr. Addison has taken the office in Mount Desert Block, formerly occupied by Mr. Heard.

Wiswell, King & Peters,
ATTORNEYS AND
COUNSELORS AT LAW
NOTARY PUBLIC.
OFFICES AT ELLSWORTH & BAR HARB

Bar Harbor Office in Mt. Desert Blo

A. P. Wiswell, A. W. King, J. A. Peters,

HALE & HAMLIN
ATTORNEYS AND
COUNSELORS AT LAW.
Offices at Ellsworth and Bar Harbor.
Land Office of the Bingham Est
H. E. Hamlin, Agent.

Bar Harbor Office,
ROOM 1,   BUNKER BLOC
Eugene Hale. Hannibal E. Hamli

J. T. HINCH, D. D. S
* * *
GRADUATE OF PHILADEL
DENTAL COLLEGE.
* * *
Rogers Building, Main

GEO. H. PREBLE.
General House Pa n
—AND—
PAPER HANGER

Three years in the employ of V
McPherson, Tremont St., Boston. N
pains will be spared to make a
my work satisfactory.

Shop, Cor. School & South Sts.

✳ ✳ ✳

	Page.		
Introduction,	3	Public Conveniences,	75
Bird's-eye View of Bar Harbor and Frenchman's Bay,	5	Sewerage, Fire and Water Systems,	7
The naming of Mount Desert Island,	9	Hints to Visitors,	
Grant of Acadia to Sieur De Monts,	9	Amusements—Their Variety—Walks,	1
Landing of the Jesuit Fathers,	10	Duck Brook Glen,	
Argall Lays Waste the French settlement,	12	Ascent of Newport Mountain. View from " "	34, 35
Norse and Indian Remains on Mount Desert,	13	The Shore Path,	37
		Driving,	38
The Second French Grant,	16	The Green Mountain Drive,	40
The De Gregoire,	17	The Ocean Drive,	41
Birth of a Summer Resort,	19	Cornice Drive,	43
Topography of Bar Harbor,	23	Twenty-two Mile Drive,	44
Boating,	47	Somesville Drive,	
Fishing,	49	Jordan's Pond,	
Society Life,	51	Green Mountain Railroad,	
Cottages,	54	Meteorological Summary—August, 1889,	
Cottages,	59	Height of Mountains,	
" H ",	62	Mount Desert—A Poem,	10
out to	65	Her Letter — A Bar Harbor Rhyme,	
from Bar Harbor,	67	Blaine's Arrival—"There is but one Bar Harbor,	
Churches,	69		

✳ ILLUSTRATIONS. ✳

✳ ✳ ✳

	Page.		Page
View from Newport House Verandah,	2	A Canoe Party,	46
Thunder Cave,	8	Mrs. R. B. Scott's Cottage, "Thirlstane,"	
A Gala Day at Bar Harbor,	15	Kebo Valley Club House,	52
A Tow Path Scene,	18	Mrs. John Whittaker's Cottage, "The Moorings,"	55
Bar Harbor from Rodick's Island,	22	Piazza of "Stanwood," Hon. James G. Blaine's cottage,	78
Mount Desert Reading Room,	26	Congregational church,	68
Devilstone Cottage and Vanderbilt Family,	30	St. Sylvia, Catholic church,	70
View of Bar Harbor and Green Mountain,	36	Unitarian church,	73
St. Saviour's Episcopal Church,	42	Methodist church,	74

www.ingramcontent.com/pod-product-compliance
Lightning Source LLC
Chambersburg PA
CBHW020125170426
43199CB00009B/644